West Sussex

40 Coast & Country Walks

The author and publisher have made every effort to ensure that the information in this publication is accurate, and accept no responsibility whatsoever for any loss, injury or inconvenience experienced by any person or persons whilst using this book.

published by
pocket mountains ltd
The Old Church, Annanside,
Moffat DG10 9HB

ISBN: 978-1-916739-02-4

Text and photography copyright © Ben Giles 2024

The right of Ben Giles to be identified as the Author of this work has been asserted by him in accordance with the Copyright, Designs and Patents Act 1988

A catalogue record for this book is available from the British Library

Contains Ordnance Survey data © Crown copyright and database 2024 supported by out of copyright mapping 1945-1961

All rights reserved. No part of this publication may be reproduced, stored in a retrieval system, or transmitted in any form or by any means, electronic or mechanical, including photocopying and recording, unless expressly permitted by Pocket Mountains Ltd.

Printed by J Thomson Colour Printers, Glasgow

Introduction

In 1911 the writer Hilaire Belloc published a novel entitled *The Four Men*, which describes a journey on foot across Sussex by four characters in late October and early November 1902. Belloc had spent much of his childhood in the Sussex village of Slindon and in 1907 had moved to King's Land in Shipley, south of Horsham. In the book's preface the narrator, called Myself, explains how he has been moved to put into words his love for 'that part of earth which nourished his boyhood' and he duly sets off to see his own land once more. But his plan to walk the county from end to end is also motivated by the impending fear that the particular nature and character of Sussex is under threat of decay, imperiled not least by 'towns of the London sort' where 'the more one worked, the less one had'.

Myself and his companions, the philosophic Grizzlebeard, the breezy Sailor and the melancholic Poet, tramp across the landscape from Robertsbridge in the east to Harting in the west. Along the way they reveal details about their different lives, swap stories from their varied experiences, recount myths and argue their opinions. On the five-day journey, which covers the period over Hallowe'en, All Saints Day and All Souls Day, they philosophise about the ills of the world and dispute various ways of living. However, throughout their time together, a sort of pilgrimage, what unites them is an affinity with the woods, streams, downs and villages through which they pass. Belloc has the characters regularly find common ground and they frequently resort to song to lighten the mood. The most famous example is when Sailor sings the First Drinking Song, with its opening line 'On Sussex hills where I was bred', while on Hallowe'en Belloc has the narrator eulogise, albeit in exaggerated manner, about 'this Eden which is still Sussex' and Grizzlebeard even imagines that the county will remain untouched at the Day of Judgment.

Quite what these characters would have made of the changes in the landscape of the last 100 years is perhaps predictable, not least their likely reaction to the growth of towns, traffic and tourism. However, if Hilaire Belloc were alive today to once more retrace the steps described at the end of the four men's journey and head alone up the steep slope of Harting's downs and on to the groves above Lavington, he would still find the essence of his words holds true: that eastward and westward stretch the wall of the Downs, southward is the belt of the sea, and northward far below sweeps the Weald.

About this guide
This guide contains 40 routes ranging in length from an hour's stroll to a day's walking, divided into five sections broadly based on the topography of the county. All of the routes are circular and are

intended as comfortable walks or strolls. On some routes, the cumulative ascent or some steeper escarpments of the downs may require greater exertion than the strict route length suggests, but in general the walking is on well-worn paths, lanes and tracks, with plenty of waymarks that should require minimal time and effort for route-finding. The route descriptions concentrate on the salient points of navigation, but may not cover every twist or turn. If in doubt, the obvious path is usually the line to take. In addition, the accompanying sketch maps serve an illustrative purpose and, for the longer or more complex routes, it would be a good idea to have access to the relevant OS Explorer mapping, details of which are given at the start of each walk.

The recommended time for each walk is an estimate based on an average walking speed of 4kmph, with a small allowance added in on some hillier routes. However, timings will vary significantly, not only for individuals but also given the seasonal effects on paths, especially those crossing fields, or tracks on the downs, sections of which can become muddier and more slippery at certain times of year.

A few routes also pass along tidal rivers or sections of coastline which can become inaccessible depending on the state of the tide. Most paths covered in these routes are well-used and well-maintained by local agencies but, in spring and summer especially, hedges and undergrowth can grow vigorously and nettles, brambles and thorn can infiltrate narrower paths, stile crossings and gates. Signage of rights of way in West Sussex is generally very good, particularly on waymarked routes such as the South Downs Way, the Serpent Trail, the Monarch's Way and the Sussex Border Path.

It is hoped that there is plenty of interest along the routes themselves and it would be possible to spread a short walk over half a day if time is taken to explore along the way. Conversely, some of the routes are short enough to attempt two in a day. In addition, this volume's companion *East Sussex: 40 Coast and Country Walks* provides further scope for exploring the region on foot.

Getting around and access

Many of the towns in West Sussex can serve as useful bases for walking. In the north of the county, the main towns are Midhurst, Billingshurst, Horsham and Crawley. In the east, close to the border with East Sussex, lie the busy commuter towns of East Grinstead, Haywards Heath and Burgess Hill, while to the west just over the county border in Hampshire is the market town of Petersfield. The county town is the city of Chichester and it serves well as a gateway to the section of the South Downs that runs to its north from Petersfield to Arundel, which itself is also well-placed for exploring the Downs.

The city provides an historic setting for exploring the extensive waters of Chichester Harbour and the low-lying peninsula of Selsey Bill to the south. Strung out along the built-up south coast of West Sussex are the busy seaside towns of Bognor Regis, Littlehampton and Worthing, whose beaches are still immensely popular with daytrippers and holidaymakers.

There is just one short section of motorway, the M23, in West Sussex and the A23, A24 and A27, the major routes in the east and south of the county, can become very busy at peak times and during holidays.

A good number of the main towns in the east of the county have railway stations, with three main railway routes: the Brighton Main Line from London, the Arun Valley Line and the West Coastway Line, which provides a regular service along the south coast between Southampton, Portsmouth, Chichester and Brighton. However, away from the coast the western half of the county is less well-served and access by train for walkers is limited to Chichester, with other stations just over the county border at Haslemere and Petersfield.

Regular bus routes serve all the main towns and, in particular, several services along the south coast are useful for walkers. An effort has been made to start walks from places which are served by public transport and, in addition, it would usually be possible to plan the completion of a walk from a town to coincide with train times. It is worth noting that it is increasingly the case that many villages in rural areas are only intermittently served by public bus on a weekly or seasonal basis.

Access by car is still the preferred option for many and, while towns cater adequately for parking, this can be a sensitive issue in smaller villages and hamlets. Pubs and inns can be very accommodating if the intention is to visit before or after a walk, but where parking is outside designated car parks consideration should be shown for the needs and access of local residents and the farming community.

West Sussex is still substantially a rural county, at least away from the conurbation along its southern coast, and has traditionally been associated with mixed farming. At lambing time, signs on gates may request that dogs are kept on leads and the presence of dogs for cows can be problematic – it is not unheard of for cows with calves to behave in a very protective way. Even without a dog, cattle just released from winter shelters or cows which have recently calved should be left well alone. If in doubt, it is usually advisable and possible to find a short detour to avoid such livestock.

Stedham Bridge over the River Rother ▶

The market town of Midhurst stands at the junction of the A286 and the A272, the two main routes in the far northwestern part of the county, and makes an excellent base for exploring. There is plenty to see in or near the town itself, not least its medieval marketplace, its Norman castle mound and the nearby ruins of Cowdray, a Tudor mansion, beside the River Rother. To the north Woolbeding Common rises to its high point at Older Hill, while further north near the border with Surrey is Black Down, the highest point in Sussex, renowned for its Temple of the Winds viewpoint. To the west of Midhurst lie the picturesque villages of Stedham and Iping and their open commons, now managed by Sussex Wildlife Trust. Heading eastwards from Midhurst towards Petworth is a high ridge on which are located the villages of Lodsworth and Tillington. Further to the south lies the northern escarpment of the South Downs and the villages of Cocking and South Harting, both of which make for satisfying start points for some higher-level walking routes.

Around Midhurst

1. Black Down and the Temple of the Winds — 8
Tennyson found daily inspiration at the viewpoint reached on this high-level circuit

2. Woolbeding Common and Older Hill — 10
You may well spot Belted Galloway cattle grazing on the upper slopes of this ancient common

3. Stedham and Iping villages — 12
This short walk near Midhurst is perfect for walking the dog or as an outing for youngsters

4. Iping and Stedham Common — 14
Weave your way with the Serpent Trail through a heathland nature reserve

5. Midhurst — 16
Midhurst is a town full of surprises, including a Norman castle mound and a ruined Tudor mansion

6. Lodsworth and Tillington — 18
Don't forget to pay your respects as you pass St Peter's Well – it's a site for sore eyes

7. Harting Down and Beacon Hill — 20
This walk to the top of the downs is short enough to leave plenty of time to explore the delightful village of South Harting

8. Cocking Down — 22
Follow the South Downs Way and byways to take in a chalk stone artwork and the Cocking History Column

Black Down and the Temple of the Winds

Distance 12km **Time** 3 hours 30
Terrain lanes, fields and open heathland, with a cumulative climb of 300m
Map OS Explorer OL33 **Access** bus to Haslemere from Farnham and Guildford; trains to Haslemere from Guildford

This higher-level walk takes you over the county border from the southern edge of the Surrey Hills to the highest point in Sussex. Queen Victoria's Poet Laureate, Alfred Lord Tennyson, is said to have walked to the Temple of the Winds viewpoint from his home at nearby Aldworth House almost every day.

From the top of the High Street in the centre of Haslemere by the town hall and war memorial, head left in the direction of Petworth along the B2131 Petworth Road. After 150m, turn left onto the footpath down Collards Lane into the National Trust-owned land of Swan Barn Farm. As the lane bends right, you join the Serpent Trail (Tail Route) whose waymarks are followed for the majority of the walk. The trail heads to the end of the lane and then along the left-hand edge of two fields to a gate into woodland. You now turn right through Witley Copse, over a track and up the left-hand edge of the wood to reach Petworth Road again.

A short dogleg left, then right takes you onto a bridleway down Pine Springs Valley. This lane, initially tarmac, descends to gates to Lythehill Estate and then forks left down a rough lane and through woodland to cross a stream in a dip. You then climb to a gate at the top of the wood and up the field beyond to High Barn Farm. Continue along the driveway to a gate, where the Serpent Trail bends left and rises steadily between fields and alongside woodland, with views left over the Surrey Hills, to meet Tennyson's Lane.

Turn right here and follow the steep wooded lane uphill for the next 800m to

BLACK DOWN AND THE TEMPLE OF THE WINDS

◂ Looking eastwards from the Temple of the Winds

the sharp right-hand bend. Keep on round the bend for 200m to the main National Trust car park on Black Down. Here, the Serpent Trail turns left past the car park and then a triangulation pillar and information board. It's now a simple task to follow the Serpent Trail waymarks for the next 1.5km over Black Down and through the woods to the viewpoint at the Temple of the Winds.

From the Temple of the Winds and its topograph pointing out the views over the South Downs, the Serpent Trail circles back sharp right (take care not to stray to the left downhill) and heads back over the western side of the top of Black Down on a clear path. After 700m, you pass a topograph and some benches to take in the views westwards before descending to a bridleway junction with the Sussex Border Path.

The Serpent Trail turns left here to head northwestwards with the Sussex Border Path across the top of Black Down, then down its western slopes and through light woodland before bending to the right and contouring northwards to a gate. The trail then leads down through Chase Wood and curves left to a gate into fields. Bear right across the first field and sharp left down the edge of the second to a gate at the bottom. The Serpent Trail now descends to a lane and continues to the right down the lane past Valewood Farm House before bending left along a track to a stream by Stedlands Farm.

Leave the Serpent Trail here and turn right past Stedlands Farm. In another 50m make sure you fork left onto a byway into woodland which heads steeply uphill to Scotland Lane. A short dogleg left along the lane, then right takes you onto a fenced footpath for 500m between gardens and the recreation ground, over Hill Road and down steps to bring you out onto Petworth Road again. Turn left along the pavement to return to the centre of Haslemere.

Woolbeding Common and Older Hill

Distance 5km **Time** 1 hour 30
Terrain mostly well-waymarked paths through woodland and over open common, with one steep ascent; low-lying sections can be boggy
Map OS Explorer OL33 **Access** no public transport to the start

Wander through woods and heathland before heading for the high vantage point of Older Hill.

The walk starts from the National Trust's Marsh Hill car park on Linch Road, a little beyond the entrance to Linch Old Rectory, 3km north of Woolbeding. Woolbeding Common is an area of hilly heathland to the north of the Rother Valley and is now owned by the National Trust. The upper parts of the heathland contain drier, sandy soils culminating in the magnificent viewpoint of Older Hill on the Greensand Ridge. The lower-lying areas mark a contrast and are far wetter, with many streams and dells. Dogs are welcome but it's worth noting that the heath is a habitat for adders. Belted Galloway cattle are also present and graze on the slopes of the common in summer to help keep the woodland scrub from becoming dominant.

Head out of the back of the small car park and follow the footpath downhill through a copse to the bridleway junction just before Woolhouse Farm. Turn right onto the bridleway, which descends gently northwards through woodland for 500m, which can be muddy at times, and then bends left across Stedham Marsh up to a junction with a restricted byway.

Turn right up the byway for 400m to a track junction at a grassy clearing by houses at Titty Hill. Continue round the right bend and join the route of the Serpent Trail (Tail Route), whose waymarks are followed to the top of the common. After 30m the Serpent Trail

◀ Near the top of Older Hill

forks right off the byway onto a public footpath through light woodland. After 250m, at the next junction, fork right and after another 200m, at a third junction, dogleg right, then immediately left to stay on the Serpent Trail, which soon heads up through woods to Linch Road.

Cross the road onto the footpath which heads up the surfaced driveway opposite for just under 200m to the entrance to Hookland Farmhouse. The trail now turns right up to Barnetts Cottage, where you take the second footpath on the left and head up past the cottage and along the side of a wooded valley. After 250m, the Serpent Trail turns left off the public right of way onto a path which climbs steeply up the open bracken- and tree-covered slope and then bears right to the triangulation pillar on Older Hill at the head of the valley. There are far-reaching views back out over the Weald here.

Continue along the path around the head of the valley to a lane, which takes you in another 250m to Older Hill car park and its viewpoint. The final part of the walk heads down the narrow winding lane for another 800m to a crosspaths where the lane bends left. Turn right here and follow the path downhill to Linch Road and the start.

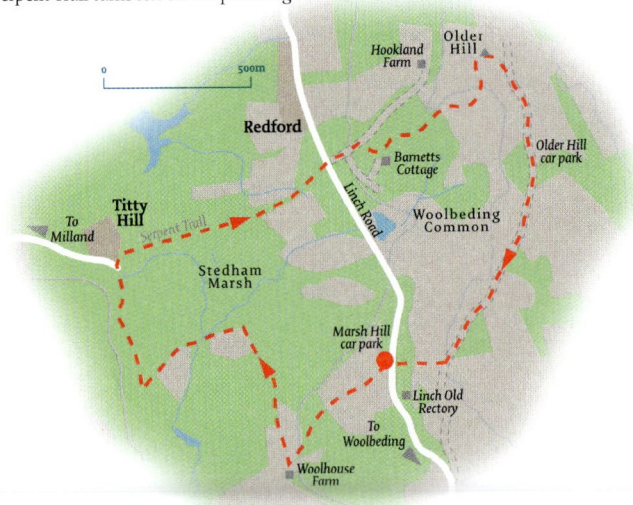

Stedham and Iping villages

Distance 4.5km **Time** 1 hour 15
Terrain lanes and footpaths over fields and through woods by the River Rother
Map OS Explorer OL33 **Access** bus to Stedham from Midhurst and Petersfield

Take a stroll between two pretty villages with plenty of local history to take in along the way.

The walk starts in the village of Stedham, where roadside parking is available. Walk along to the northern end of the village and fork right along Mill Lane, which carries a footpath, past the timber-framed Tye Hill to St James' Church, where you can see a large yew tree, thought to be about 2500 years old. The church itself was substantially rebuilt in the middle of the 19th century, when the nave and chancel were realigned north of the tower, and you can still see the outline of the original Saxon building on the west side of the tower. To the right of the porch are a stone coffin and some gravestones which are thought to be pre-Saxon.

Continue along the lane round the left bend, past the entrance to Stedham Hall and some cottages, and then between fields down to Stedham Mill. Bear left in front of the house and cross over the River Rother and between the ponds to a footpath junction. Keep ahead into the trees and uphill along a sunken path to Stedham Lane.

A left turn takes you along this twisting and undulating lane for 400m to a junction at a bend. Keep ahead along Stanwater Lane, signed for Iping and rising gently uphill to Crouchhouse Farm. Continue past the farmhouse and head down round the left bend to a

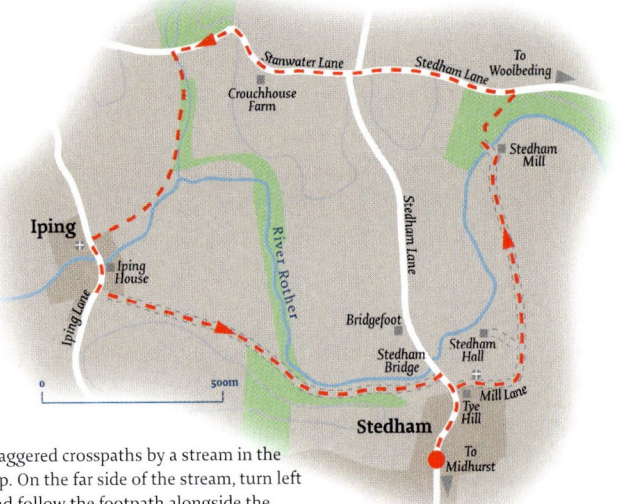

staggered crosspaths by a stream in the dip. On the far side of the stream, turn left and follow the footpath alongside the edges of two fields to Iping Lane, opposite St Mary's Church in Iping village.

The final part of the walk turns left along Iping Lane over the bridge across the River Rother. The narrowness of the bridge gives the clue that in origin it was constructed for packhorse traffic. On the right was the site of Iping Mill, which was first a cornmill, then a papermill and finally one of the earliest to produce blotting paper. A cottage on the site is still called The Blotting House.

Continue round the bend past Iping House and, after another 50m, turn left onto a bridleway up an old cobbled path and along a driveway past cottages. The bridleway now forks right off the driveway and continues up between a garden and a field, over a small rise and down between fields into woodland. Keep ahead through the trees beside the River Rother to Stedham Bridge. A right turn here uphill along Stedham Lane will take you back into the village.

However, it's worth detouring left to the middle of the bridge for a view up to Stedham Hall. In origin the house is Tudor, but its more modern appearance dates from the beginning of the 20th century when John Scrimgeour, a local benefactor, inherited it and set about giving it a neo-Tudor look, with a stone ground floor and half-timbered upper storeys. Scrimgeour provided housing for the village as well as improved amenities, including pumped water, and is commemorated by a plaque in St James' Church. The hall, along with its estate, was sold off in the 1950s and converted into apartments.

◀ St James' Church, Stedham

Iping and Stedham Common

Distance 4.75km **Time** 1 hour 15
Terrain clear and mostly well-waymarked paths over heathland and through woods
Map OS Explorer OL33 **Access** bus from Midhurst and Petersfield stops on the A272 opposite Iping Lane, 250m from the start

There's plenty of flora and fauna to spot on this varied route over heathland and through woods.

The walk starts from the Iping and Stedham Commons Nature Reserve car park on Elsted Road, 250m from the A272, 4km west of Midhurst. These commons are an extensive area of lowland heathland and are managed by Sussex Wildlife Trust. The dry acidic conditions of the soil are ideal for heather, birch, gorse, Scots pine and purple moor grass. Rare breed cattle are put out to pasture on the commons and help to control the balance of the vegetation, essential for heath-loving birds such as the woodlark and Dartford warbler. The heath is also an ideal habitat for adders and you might just see one basking in early sunshine. Dogs are welcome and owners are asked to keep them under close control, especially during the ground-nesting season between March and September.

Walk through the gate at the back of the car park and, at the junction beyond, fork right along the bridleway on the route of the Serpent Trail (Tail Route), which is followed for the first part of the walk. Follow the waymarked Serpent Trail westwards for 750m over the heathland of Iping Common, which is predominantly covered here with heather, bracken, gorse and silver birch, over a bridleway crosspaths and gently up to a second bridleway crosspaths just before the top of the rise.

The Serpent Trail turns left along the bridleway down to a gate, where it turns

◂ Looking towards the South Downs from Fitzhall Plantation

left again onto a sandy bridleway leading down the heath beside the former plantation of Goldrings Warren on the right. At the bottom of Goldrings Warren, fork left with the Serpent Trail down through woodland. After 250m, the Serpent Trail turns off right onto a footpath but this route continues along the bridleway to Elsted Road.

Cross the road and follow the bridleway opposite initially along the edge of and then through Fitzhall Plantation, where you walk gently uphill over a rise and down to the driveway for Fitzhall. Cross over the driveway and continue along the track opposite, which carries the bridleway. The track soon bends right and heads down through some sandstone outcrops, after which it bends left by a house to a bridleway junction.

Keep left and follow the bridleway up between fields and into mixed woodland to a second bridleway junction. Fork right here and continue through the woodland and then between fields on the right and a flooded sandpit on the left, which is screened from view by trees, to Minsted Road. Turn left here up the dead-straight lane for just under 500m to the top of the rise and take the bridleway off left onto the Serpent Trail once more. This rises gently through woodland and for the final 500m heads over the heath beyond back to Elsted Road and the car park.

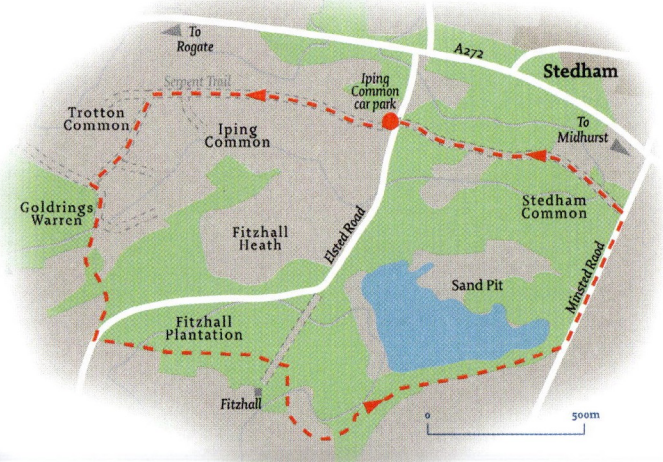

Midhurst

Distance 7.5km **Time** 2 hours
Terrain well-waymarked paths through fields, woods and beside the River Rother (this section can be muddy and is prone to flooding) **Map** OS Explorer OL33
Access bus to Midhurst from Chichester, Worthing and Petersfield

This jewel of a country walk winds its way past ruins, beside the River Rother and over Midhurst Common.

From the centre of Midhurst, by the roundabout at the junction of the A272 with the A286, head down West Street to Market Square, where you'll find the Parish Church of St Mary Magdalene and St Denys, as well as the Old Town Hall with its stocks and pillory. Pass through the square and along St Anne's Hill to a gate. The route forks left in front of the mound of Midhurst Castle, where there are some useful information boards to help interpret the site of this early Norman fortification. The hill is currently covered in trees but originally there would have been a clear and strategic view over the surrounding land and the River Rother, once an important means of transporting people and goods.

Continue past the castle mound and go down steps to the River Rother. Keep ahead alongside the river and round the left bend to the bridge opposite Cowdray, once a great Tudor mansion and now one of the most impressive ruins of the period. Cross the bridge and turn left along the driveway through Cowdray Park, which carries a footpath, to the A272.

Turn left here over the roadbridge's pedestrian walkway and then turn right onto the permissive Rother Walk path. The route follows the waymarks of this path for a little under 2km, initially meandering alongside the river and then

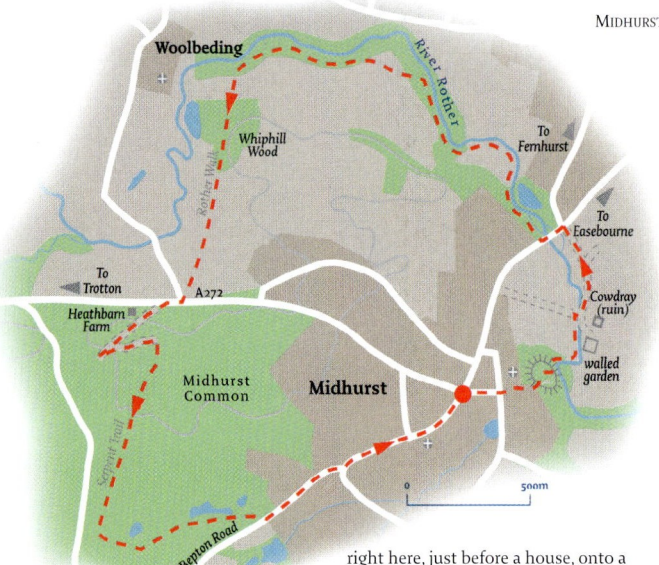

along a section of boardwalk. You then head along the edges of two fields to a gate into the National Trust-owned Woolbeding Parkland. From here, the Rother Walk heads to the left up the parkland, through Whiphill Wood and then over another large field to the A272.

At this point, you leave the Rother Walk, cross the road and take the footpath 30m to the right up a track through deciduous woodland and into a conifer plantation. Just before the track bends left, the footpath forks right (ahead) and after another 50m reaches a triple-forked path junction. Turn sharp left onto the Serpent Trail (Head Route) and follow the waymarks back up to the track and along it again for 30m. The Serpent Trail forks right here, just before a house, onto a narrow path up through the trees to the next junction, where it turns right.

The trail now heads downhill alongside the edge of conifers on the right and then follows the line of the telegraph poles with the gorse, silver birch and heather of Midhurst Common on the left. After 800m the trail turns left with the electricity lines to a bridleway junction. Keep ahead through an embankment and bend left with the bridleway for a pleasant 500m through deciduous woodland to Bepton Road.

You now leave the Serpent Trail and turn left along the walkway and then the pavement on the far side of the road. Continue past the recycling centre up to the junction with the A286, which leads you back down into Midhurst.

◀ The ruins of Cowdray

Lodsworth and Tillington

Distance 9km **Time** 2 hours 30
Terrain lanes, fields and woodland
Map OS Explorer OL33 **Access** bus to
Tillington from Midhurst and Worthing
stops just off the route on the A272 at the
bottom of Upperton Road

Enjoy a varied walk between two attractive villages along the sandstone ridge to the west of Petworth Park.

The walk starts from the centre of the village of Lodsworth, where there is limited parking by Lodsworth Larder, the village shop, or at the recreation ground by the village hall, situated 300m along Gills Lane/Heath End Lane. Walk down The Street to the bend a little beyond Vicarage Lane and Woodmancote, a house with a blue plaque commemorating its former resident, the artist E H Shepard, illustrator of *Winnie-the-Pooh* and *The Wind in the Willows*. Turn left down Church Lane to St Peter's Church. The church contains the Lodsworth Tapestry, which depicts life in the village during the 20th century, and from the churchyard, where E H Shepard is buried, there is a good view to the 14th-century Manor House.

Past the church at the bottom of the lane, fork right onto a bridleway and head past St Peter's Well, which was once a popular place of pilgrimage for those with eye problems and likely predates the church. Just beyond the well, the bridleway turns right down a field into woodland to Eel Bridge and the River Lod. At the path junction across the bridge, fork right and follow the bridleway uphill, where it zigzags left and then right to meet River Lane.

The route now turns right and follows the narrow lane for the next 1.5km, heading gently uphill past Standlands, over the rise and down across Dene Dip to New Road. Cross the road and take the public footpath ahead past vineyards,

◂ St Peter's Church, Lodsworth

across a sunken way and then between fields to Cemetery Lane in Tillington.

Turn left and follow the lane up past the cemetery and through the village to Upperton Road. Opposite is All Hallows Church with its striking 'Scots Crown' spire. It is the most southerly example of its kind in Britain and was built by Lord Egremont in 1807 as a landmark on the western edge of his Petworth Estate.

From here, head left up Upperton Road for the next 1.25km alongside the estate wall of Petworth Park and through the village of Upperton to the junction above the last house at the edge of Upperton Common. Turn left here, signed for Pitshill, and at the bend after 250m keep ahead onto a bridleway.

You soon pass a lodgehouse and join the Sussex Diamond Way, whose waymarks are followed for the rest of the walk. Continue down through the wood to a path junction below the house of Pitshill. Here, leave the bridleway, which turns right, and follow the Diamond Way ahead onto a footpath which gradually descends the steep southern side of Upperton Common through woods, mostly of beech. After 1km, at a crosspaths with a sunken public way, cross and keep on downhill to River Lane.

The Diamond Way turns left along the lane for 100m, then turns right down between gardens and bends left into woodland again. After another 250m, look out for a marker post where the Sussex Diamond Way forks right onto a narrower path down to Eel Bridge. From here, retrace your steps up past St Peter's Well to the start.

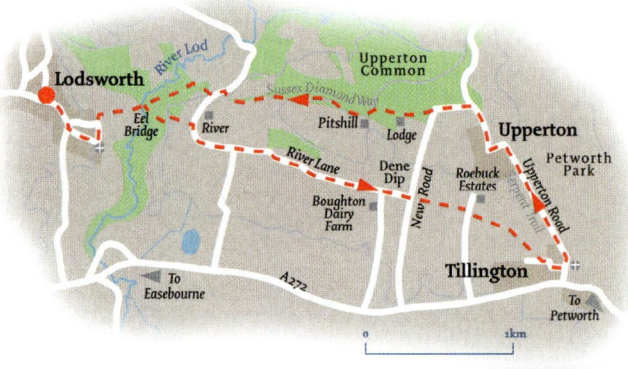

Harting Down and Beacon Hill

Distance 7.25km **Time** 2 hours 15
Terrain woods, fields and open
downland, with some steep gradients
Map OS Explorer OL33
Access bus to South Harting from
Chichester and Petersfield

Some fine views are the reward on this straightforward but energetic climb to an historic viewpoint.

The walk starts from the village of South Harting by the Church of St Mary and St Gabriel, where you can see the old village stocks and, in the churchyard, Harting War Memorial, the work of the sculptor Eric Gill and his assistant Desmond Chute. Its design is reminiscent of a medieval cross and, as well as the fine lettering, carved in low relief around the base are the patron saints of England (St George), Ireland (St Patrick), Scotland (St Andrew) and Wales (St David). Of particular interest inside the church are the Caryll and Cowper family tombs and a modern sculpture *The Archangel Gabriel*, by the renowned sculptor Philip Jackson, a resident of nearby Cocking whose many public commissions include the Bomber Command Memorial in London's Green Park and the statue of Bobby Moore at Wembley Stadium.

Head past the church along the narrow section of road and, at the bend, fork right onto a footpath past a small parking area into South Gardens and The Warren. The footpath heads along the left side of the gardens and continues uphill, initially steeply, through the woodland of The Warren to the B2146.

Cross the road and join the South Downs Way which heads gently up through woodland for 800m to the B2141. Cross over and head past the National Trust car park onto Harting Down, where there are good views northwards over South Harting towards Black Down and

HARTING DOWN AND BEACON HILL

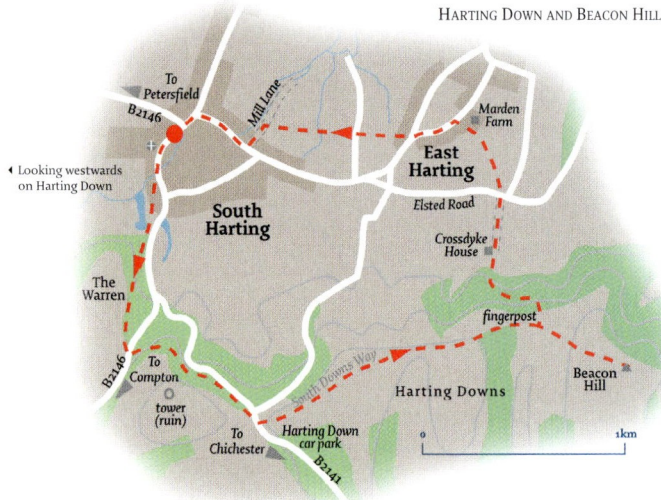

◄ Looking westwards on Harting Down

the Surrey Hills. For the next 1.5km, the South Downs Way heads ENE along the left-hand of two bridleways over the northern escarpment of Harting Down and descends to a five-way path junction in the prominent dip below Beacon Hill.

From here, ready yourself for a steep climb up the western slope of Beacon Hill to its triangulation pillar and memorial topograph, from where there are views south to Portsmouth and the Isle of Wight. Beacon Hill, along with its eastern neighbour, Pen Hill, is the site of a prehistoric enclosure dating back almost 3000 years to the late Bronze Age, while the south side of the hill is the location of an Anglo-Saxon burial site, now levelled by ploughing. In Napoleonic times, during the threat of invasion by the French, the hill also saw the construction of a telegraph station for relaying messages from the naval base at Portsmouth to The Admiralty in London. The topograph is located on part of the foundations of this station.

To continue, retrace your steps down the western slope of the hill to the dip and take the bridleway northwards, signed for East Harting, down through a wooded combe and past Crossdyke House to the junction with Elsted Road. Cross over and follow the footpath ahead across three fields to Marden Farm, where you should bear left past its buildings to East Harting Street. Turn left down this narrow lane for 250m to the junction and then take the footpath off right back into fields. The footpath heads along a hedged section, across a lane and over two more fields to Mill Lane. Turn left here down to Elsted Road, where a right turn will take you back into South Harting.

AROUND MIDHURST

Cocking Down

Distance 6.75km **Time** 2 hours
Terrain mostly clear tracks and paths over fields and downs **Map** OS Explorer OL8
Access bus to Cocking from Midhurst and Chichester

Head up onto the South Downs Way and look out for an enigmatic chalk stone.

The walk starts from the village of Cocking, where there is some limited parking on Bell Lane along from The Blue Bell pub, now a community hub. An alternative is to start along the route at the car park on Cocking Down, located beside the A286 1km south of the village, where there is also a bus stop (South Downs Way stop).

From the centre of Cocking by the junction of Mill Lane with the A286, go down the narrow no-through lane beside the village stores to the Parish Church of St Catherine of Siena, whose Lady Chapel houses an icon of the saint. Continue over Costers Brook and take the restricted byway off to the right. This pleasant wooded track at first rises gently and then twists its way uphill a little more steeply between fields and past the buildings of Manor Farm to Hillbarn Lane. Turn right here down the hedged lane, along the route of the South Downs Way, to the A286.

Cross the road and continue along the lane opposite, past the car park, to Cocking Hill Farm and Cadence Café (those visiting the café are welcome to use their car park). From here, the route starts to head uphill and steadily gains height up the broad eastern slope of Cocking Down. At the first crosspaths you pass a large chalk stone, reminiscent of the waystones which once guided travellers on the downs. This is not a natural feature but a sculpture on the

◀ Looking eastwards past artist Andy Goldsworthy's Chalk Stone on Cocking Down

Chalk Stones Trail. There are 13 such stones, installed in 2002 between Cocking Hill and West Dean by the environmental artist Andy Goldsworthy in collaboration with Pallant House Gallery in Chichester.

Continue up the track, a little less steeply now, for another 800m to a second crosspaths. Leave the South Downs Way here and turn right onto the restricted byway which heads across the top of Stead Combe and into woodland. The byway soon bends right and starts to descend, flanked by yew trees and then beech trees with a good view northwards to the Surrey Hills. The byway, called Henley Lane, descends past the junction with the byway up from Bepton to the far edge of the trees and then continues for another 900m downhill along a hedged section to a byway T-junction (if overgrown, there is a track along the field edge to the right). There are good views ahead to the old chalk quarries on the far side of the valley above Sun Combe, which used to supply lime for Midhurst Brickworks.

At the byway T-junction, turn right down to Crypt Farm and then go left down past the farmhouse and continue along its driveway, where you pass under a brick bridge of the former Chichester to Midhurst railway line. It's another 400m back to the A286 at the southern edge of Cocking where you can make a short detour left along a footpath to Cocking History Column, which comprises a series of 48 bronze panels recording scenes from the village's history.

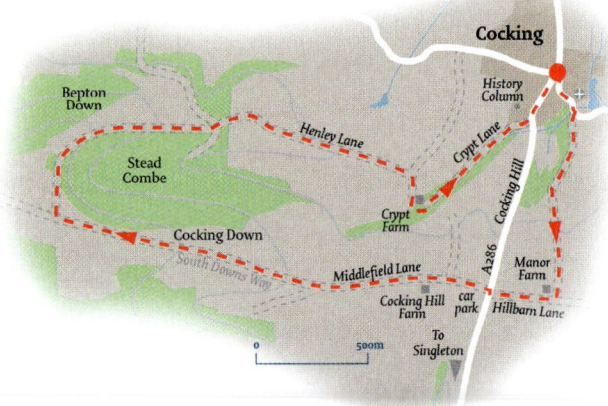

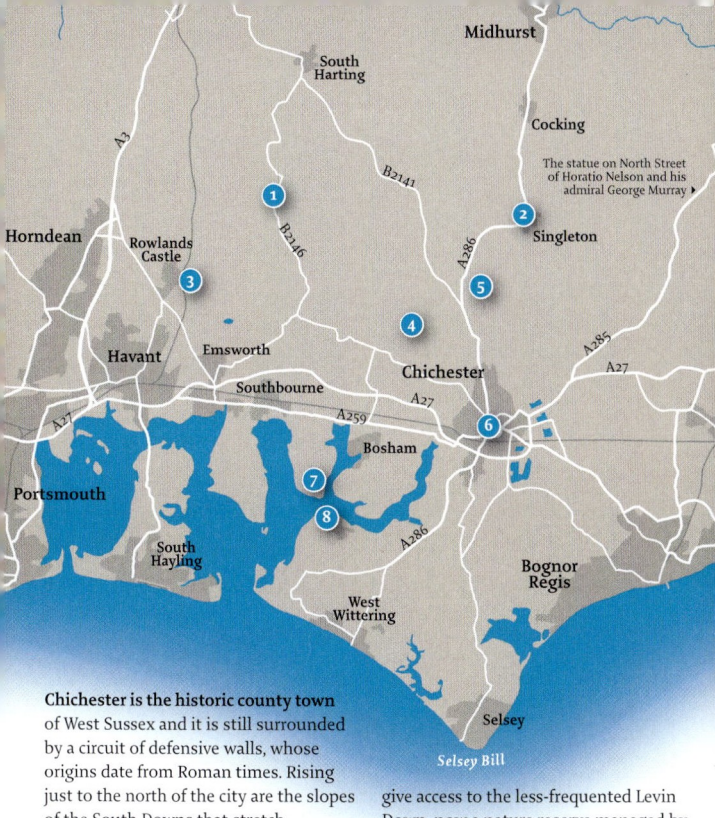

The statue on North Street of Horatio Nelson and his admiral George Murray ▶

Chichester is the historic county town of West Sussex and it is still surrounded by a circuit of defensive walls, whose origins date from Roman times. Rising just to the north of the city are the slopes of the South Downs that stretch eastwards from the county's western border with Hampshire. Here, hidden in the folds of the downs you'll find the elongated Neolithic barrow of Bevis's Thumb, the magical yew groves in Kingley Vale and the Iron Age hillfort of The Trundle above West Dean and Goodwood Racecourse. A little to the north are the villages of Singleton and Charlton which give access to the less-frequented Levin Down, now a nature reserve managed by Sussex Wildlife Trust. To the southwest of the city lie the extensive waters and tidal channels of Chichester Harbour, once busy with commercial shipping but now a haven for wildlife. Across the Chichester Channel, the village of West Itchenor lies just a short distance from the popular beaches at West Wittering and the famous promontory of Selsey Bill.

Around Chichester

1. **Compton and Bevis's Thumb** — 26
   Head out in search of the mythical resting place of the giant Bevis while enjoying far-reaching views

2. **Singleton and Levin Down** — 28
   One of Sussex's prettiest villages is the start point for this climb up chalk grassland slopes

3. **Rowlands Castle and Stansted Park** — 30
   Stride out on this delightful circuit through landscaped parkland and a remnant of ancient woodland

4. **West Stoke and Kingley Vale** — 32
   Tread gently in the footsteps of the pioneering ecologist Sir Arthur Tansley in this haven for flora and fauna

5. **West Dean and The Trundle** — 34
   Make a day of it and combine this route with a visit to nearby West Dean Gardens or the Weald and Downland Living Museum

6. **Chichester Walls** — 36
   Don't miss the Bishop's Palace Gardens and the Novium Museum on this historical circuit

7. **Chidham Peninsula and Cobnor Point** — 38
   Be sure to time it right to avoid high tide along this refreshing foreshore foray

8. **West Itchenor and Chichester Channel** — 40
   Make a pilgrimage to a church dedicated to the patron saint of seafarers on this coastal loop

Compton and Bevis's Thumb

Distance 5.75km **Time** 1 hour 45
Terrain quiet lanes, tracks and paths over fields and through woodland
Map OS Explorer OL8 **Access** bus to Compton from Chichester and Petersfield

A short steep climb takes you up onto less frequented downs where there are some long views and hidden history.

From the centre of Compton by the old well and village shop, where there is some limited parking, walk along School Lane past the school and continue up the wooded track beyond, which carries a bridleway. After 100m, you come to a three-way fork where the bridleway branches left and right. Take the footpath ahead (between the two forks of the bridleway) and climb steeply up through the trees and then along a field edge to a track. Dogleg left, then immediately right over the track onto the bridleway which heads downhill beside a strip of woodland and then down field edges to the bottom of the valley.

Continue up the far side, where the bridleway is lined by trees and banks, to a staggered crosspaths just before a gate and the hamlet of Up Marden. Look out for a marker post here showing the footpath off left along the field edge beside a wood. At the end of the wood, keep ahead along the footpath across the field and on the far side join a track which heads over the top of Apple Down and down to Long Lane. It's worth pausing on top of the down for the extensive views over to the right back to Kingley Vale, ahead to Harting Down and left to Uppark, and on the horizon the radio station mast on Butser Hill is visible on a clear day. It's also something of a surprise

COMPTON AND BEVIS'S THUMB

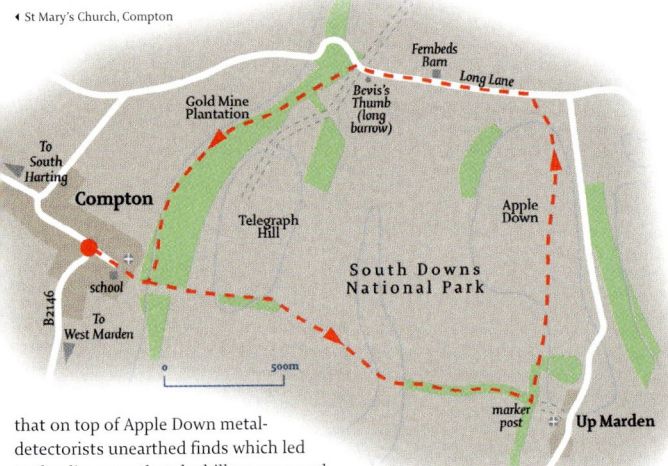

◀ St Mary's Church, Compton

that on top of Apple Down metal-detectorists unearthed finds which led to the discovery that the hilltop was used in the 5th to 7th centuries as an Anglo-Saxon cemetery. Subsequent excavations found evidence for more than 200 burials on the site, as well as about 30 timber structures which have been interpreted as houses for the dead.

Turn left and follow the lane down across the dip past Fernbeds Barn and up the far side to a bridleway crosspaths at the top of the rise. Just on the left behind the hedge at the edge of the field is an elongated barrow. It is known as Bevis's Thumb and, at 60m in length, is one of the longest burial mounds of its type in the South East. Excavations in the 1980s dated the structure to 2500BCE and established that it was originally surrounded by ditches. This feature is no longer visible and, on the northern side, is covered by the road. The name may refer to the giant of a man who was once the Warden at Arundel Castle, where there is a Bevis Tower. From its battlements, Bevis hurled his sword and the place where it fell marked the spot for his burial.

The final part of the route turns left off the lane past the western end of the barrow and then takes the right-hand of the two bridleways downhill along the field edge. Continue down through Gold Mine Plantation for a little under 1.5km to the three-way path junction encountered on the outward route. A right turn here takes you back down into Compton, where you can take the narrow path off right just before the bottom of the track to see St Mary's Church, which has an attractive timber turret and spire.

Singleton and Levin Down

Distance 5km (including short detour into Charlton) **Time** 1 hour 30 **Terrain** field paths and tracks over the downs **Map** OS Explorer OL8 **Access** bus to Singleton from Chichester and Midhurst

Amble over fields between two picturesque villages before circling back over the slopes of a nature reserve.

The walk starts from the village of Singleton, where there is some limited roadside parking available. From the crossroads of Charlton Road and Cobbler's Row in the middle of the village by The Partridge Inn, walk down the lane opposite that leads to St Mary's Church. By Church Cottage take the footpath off left, signed for Charlton, past the church. Devotees of work inspired by the Italian Baroque sculptor Bernini may wish to call in to the church to see the reredos, carved from Caen stone by the 19th-century Scottish sculptor James Forsyth, who was later commissioned for the reredos, choir stalls and Bishop's Throne in Chichester Cathedral. In the churchyard is buried the author Ian Serraillier, perhaps best known for his 1950s children's novel *The Silver Sword*.

Continue past the playground, through the houses on Church Way and then the housing estate beyond into fields. The footpath follows the right-hand field edge across the former watermeadows of the River Lavant to a lane on the outskirts of Charlton. Turn left to the junction with Charlton Road. From here, you can detour off right into the village. Since 1985, the pub has been called The Fox Goes Free and is a reminder that Charlton as a village is closely linked with hunting. Many of the houses were built as hunting lodges, and so too was Fox Hall, erected by the Duke of Richmond in 1731.

The onward route crosses the road and for the next 1.2km heads up North Lane, a

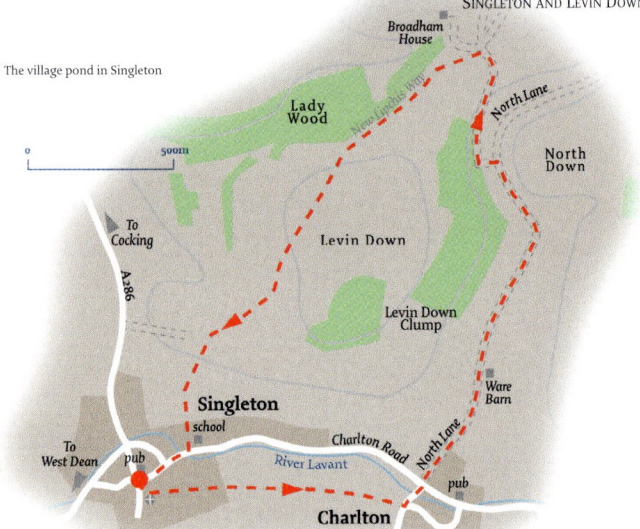

◀ The village pond in Singleton

rough hedged lane which carries a public way and rises gently between fields, past Ware Barn and round a left bend to a prominent bridleway junction. Leave North Lane here and turn left onto the bridleway which soon bends right and rises more steeply up the wooded east side of Levin Down to a five-way path junction.

Follow the bridleway round to the left, signed for Singleton, and go through the gate onto the Access Land of Levin Down. In Old English the name *Levin* means 'Leave-Alone' and refers to the fact that no crops were grown on it. Today, the hill is a nature reserve owned by the Goodwood Estate and managed by Sussex Wildlife Trust. The route now follows the bridleway, which carries the New Lipchis Way, over the right-hand side of the down for 600m to a gate in the fence. Turn left off the bridleway, which continues through the gate, and head up alongside the fence over the shoulder of the down to a second gate, where there is a good view on the left to The Trundle and, on a clear day, ahead to the Isle of Wight.

The final part of the walk now rejoins the bridleway and heads down the southwest side of the down to a crosspaths. After another 200m, at a fingerpost just before the limit of Access Land, bear left off the bridleway onto a footpath. Keep on downhill through two gates and down the field beyond to Charlton Road by the school, where a right turn will take you back into Singleton and the start.

Rowlands Castle and Stansted Park

Distance 9.75km **Time** 2 hours 30
Terrain paths and tracks over parkland and through woodland
Map OS Explorer OL8 **Access** bus to Rowlands Castle from Havant and Emsworth (limited service); train to Rowlands Castle from Portsmouth and London Waterloo

Wander over parkland and through the westerly remnant of the ancient hunting forest of Arundel.

The walk starts from the east end of the Green near the railway station in Rowlands Castle. The village sits right on the Hampshire/Sussex border, though Stansted Park itself is in West Sussex. In 1983, Stansted House was given to the nation by its then owner, the 10th Earl of Bessborough, and its 1800 acres of ancient forest and landscaped parkland, which in the 1780s were redesigned with the help of Lancelot 'Capability' Brown, are now managed by Stansted Park Foundation.

Walk past the cafés and shops to the railway arches and fork left along Finchdean Road for 150m to the bend. Take the footpath off right along the route of the Monarch's Way over two crosspaths and up through woodland to the start of The Avenue. Follow the footpath, which is flanked by the trees of Stansted Forest, for just over 1.5km down this long and wide grassy approach to Stansted House. The impressive façade of the current house dates from 1900 and replaced a 17th-century mansion, which was destroyed by fire. At Main Avenue/Broad Walk, cross over and take the bridleway opposite, past the neoclassical Middle Lodge, along the estate road. Follow this up through North Coopers Wood and then continue up through some bends to a bridleway junction by a

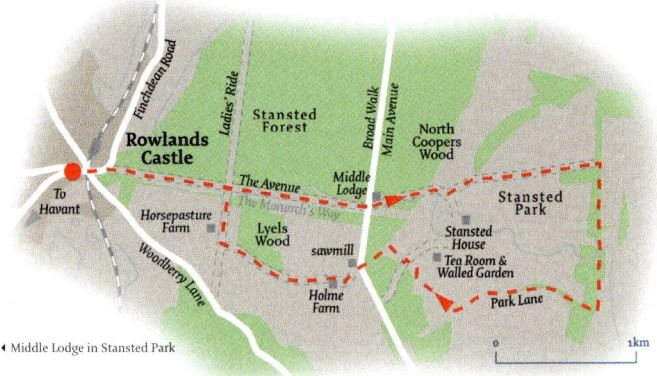

◀ Middle Lodge in Stansted Park

pair of flint-walled cottages. Fork right with the Monarch's Way off the estate road and follow the bridleway for the next 1km along a hedged track and then through woodland to a six-way junction.

Go through the double gates and turn right, off the Monarch's Way, onto the restricted byway. This leads southwards for just over 1km, gently down along the edge of woodland and up to a T-junction. Turn right down the restricted byway of Park Lane, through the trees and up to a crosspaths by a house. Continue along the byway, as it narrows, for another 350m to a staggered crosspaths. Turn right through a gate onto a footpath, which heads up between a field and a plantation before crossing another field to a gate back into woodland.

Turn right to the entrance road to Stansted House and its car park, where on the right you can access the house, its public tearoom and shops. The onward route turns left along the entrance road for 100m to the junction at the bend and then continues ahead onto a bridleway. A little way along there's a clear view to the façade of Stansted House before you swing left along the edge of South Coopers Wood and over a field to Main Avenue.

Cross over and head past the sawmill along the track to Holme Farm. After 200m, turn right onto the footpath which passes to the right of the farm buildings and then bends left along a track at their rear. Continue up between fields and along the edge of Lyels Wood to a track junction at the entrance to Horsepasture Farm. The final part of the walk turns right here and heads across the field beyond back to The Avenue, where you turn left and retrace the outward route to Rowlands Castle.

West Stoke and Kingley Vale

Distance 6km **Time** 1 hour 45
Terrain well-waymarked trail over fields and through woods with some steep sections **Map** OS Explorer OL8
Access no public transport to the start

Explore the spectacularly-shaped yew trees on the steep slopes of a popular nature reserve.

The walk starts from West Stoke car park which serves the southern entrance to Kingley Vale National Nature Reserve. The car park is located 5km northwest of Chichester along Downs Road on the western edge of West Stoke village and can become busy at peak periods. The nature reserve is a mixture of chalk grassland, scrub, and mixed oak and ash woodland. What makes Kingley Vale of particular note is that it is also one of the finest examples of ancient yew forest in Europe. However, some of the yew trees still carry the scars of bullet holes from the Second World War when the area was used by troops training for D-Day. Once in the reserve, the route follows the popular Kingley Vale Nature Trail.

At the rear of the car park, go through the gate and follow the surfaced footpath between fields for a little over 1km to the bridleway junction by the entrance gate to Kingley Vale National Nature Reserve. Go through the gate to the start of the Nature Trail, which is waymarked by numbered posts and initially shares a route with the Yew Tree Trail. The Nature Trail heads past a small field museum hut explaining the history of the vale and there are also a number of information panels along the route. You soon pass into woodland and, after 200m, fork right. The trail heads up the main path with a number of small detours off to the right where you thread your way through the yew trees.

After 600m, you emerge into a clearing below the steep head of the vale. The

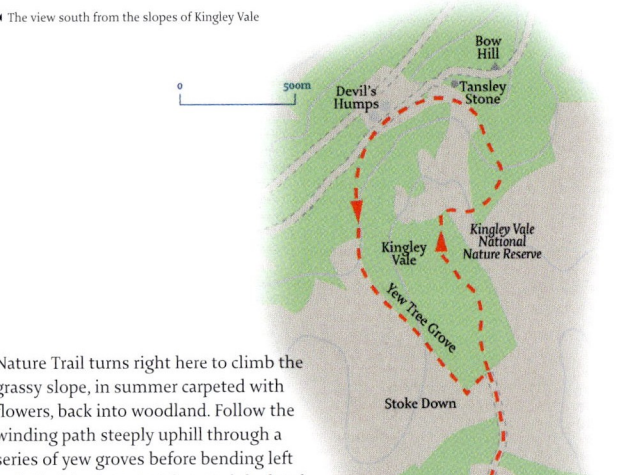

◀ The view south from the slopes of Kingley Vale

Nature Trail turns right here to climb the grassy slope, in summer carpeted with flowers, back into woodland. Follow the winding path steeply uphill through a series of yew groves before bending left and climbing less steeply round the head of the vale to a junction with a stepped path up from the bottom of the combe. At this point, you can make a short detour up to the right to see the Tansley Stone, which commemorates Sir Arthur Tansley, the pioneering ecologist who was central to establishing the nature reserve in 1952.

The onward route keeps ahead to a gate and then continues up across the grassy slope beyond towards the Devil's Humps, which date from the Bronze Age and are thought to be burial mounds for kings. The trail bends left and heads past the mounds. After 100m look out for a marker post showing the way off to the left down some steps and through a gate. From here, you descend the vale's western slope for just under 1.5km, going down through more yew groves before the trail bends round to the left to return you to the gate at the entrance to the nature reserve. From here, turn right and retrace your steps along the footpath to the car park.

West Dean and The Trundle

Distance 11.75km **Time** 3 hours 15 **Terrain** field and woodland paths, downland tracks and a former railway line **Map** OS Explorer OL8 **Access** bus to West Dean from Midhurst and Chichester

Gain a sense of history on this climb to an Iron Age hillfort with a return along the shared-use Centurion Way.

The walk starts from the village of West Dean, where parking is available on Church Lane by the green and the River Lavant. From the crossroads on the A286 in West Dean by the school, the bus stop and The Selsey Arms, walk down the lane past the village shop and café to Church Lane. Turn right and follow the lane for 150m alongside the River Lavant.

At the bend, take the bridleway which heads off left over the river and alongside the estate wall of West Dean Estate. The bridleway soon starts to climb up through some woodland and then along a field edge before passing through woodland again. At the end of the estate wall, keep ahead uphill to the far edge of the wood where you pass along a field edge and past The Rubbing House to a track junction by Trundle car park. To reach The Trundle and its views over Goodwood Racecourse and the South Downs, take the track ahead uphill for 400m and return to the car park.

The name Trundle comes from the Anglo-Saxon word *tryndel*, meaning 'a circle'. The hill was first occupied during the Neolithic period 5500 years ago. During the Iron Age, a hillfort was constructed and occupied until about 100BCE. A small medieval chapel dedicated to St Roche, a French saint prayed to in times of plague, a gibbet and also a signal beacon once stood on the hill. Today, the

WEST DEAN AND THE TRUNDLE

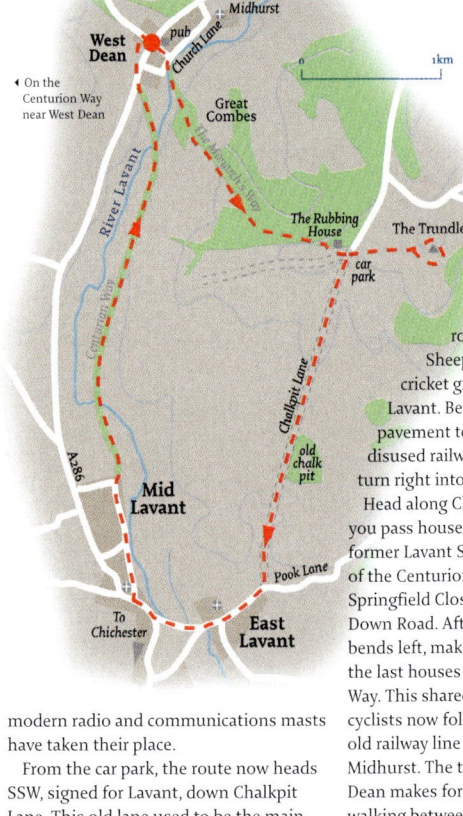

◀ On the Centurion Way near West Dean

modern radio and communications masts have taken their place.

From the car park, the route now heads SSW, signed for Lavant, down Chalkpit Lane. This old lane used to be the main road from Chichester to London. Now it's a flinty track and for the next 2.5km takes you down past an old chalkpit to Pook Lane. Turn right along the pavement through East Lavant, past St Mary's Church and over the River Lavant. At the junction just beyond, the route turns right along Sheepwash Lane past the cricket ground to the A286 in Mid Lavant. Bear right along the pavement to the bridge over the disused railway line and, just beyond, turn right into the housing estate.

Head along Churchmead Close, where you pass houses built on the site of former Lavant Station, and join the route of the Centurion Way, which heads into Springfield Close and then along Lavant Down Road. After 700m, where the road bends left, make sure you fork right past the last houses to stay on the Centurion Way. This shared route for walkers and cyclists now follows the trackbed of the old railway line from Chichester to Midhurst. The tree-lined section to West Dean makes for 3km of easy and pleasant walking between fields and up a slight incline to the short tunnel under the A286. After another 300m, look out for the marker post showing the way into West Dean, down steps on the right and along the lane past the school back to the A286 and the start.

Chichester Walls

Distance 4km **Time** 1 hour
Terrain city streets and Walls Walk
Map OS Explorer OL8 **Access** bus to Chichester from Portsmouth, Midhurst, Arundel and Littlehampton; train to Chichester from Portsmouth, Horsham and Brighton

This elevated stroll around Chichester's Roman walls will whet your appetite for exploring the rest of the city.

The walk starts from the centre of Chichester at the Market Cross near the cathedral. The route follows the City Walls Trail, which is waymarked at key points along its route by fingerposts and pavement discs. The city's origins stretch back to the Romans, who founded a market town here in the 1st century CE with the name Noviomagus Reginorum (New-market of the Regnenses tribe). The first walls around the town, along with four gateways, were constructed in the 3rd century. The Normans built a castle in the northeast quadrant and restored the walls, which remained fortified until after the Civil War in the 17th century. The walls are now a Scheduled Monument and are managed by the Chichester Walls Trust, which has placed information panels along the route to help explain the city's history.

Head up North Street past the statue of Horatio Nelson and his admiral George Murray, who was Mayor of Chichester in 1815. Just before Northgate, turn right along Priory Lane to the bend and fork left into Priory Park. Follow North East Walls Walk around the perimeter of the park, from where you gain a good view down over the Guildhall, formerly the chapel of the Franciscan Priory, and the motte of the Norman castle. Continue

Chichester Walls

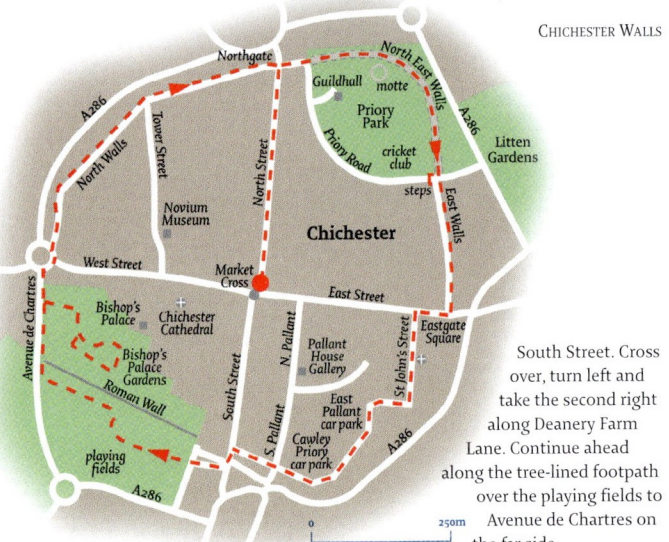

South Street. Cross over, turn left and take the second right along Deanery Farm Lane. Continue ahead along the tree-lined footpath over the playing fields to Avenue de Chartres on the far side.

along the walls past the county cricket ground and cross over Priory Road.

On the far side, head up the steps above the old gunpowder store and continue along East Walls Walk to Eastgate Square on the site of the old East Gate, whose gatehouse served as the city's first jail. The trail doglegs right along East Street and then takes the first left along St John's Street, where you pass St John's Chapel. You can also detour off right here to Pallant House Gallery and its collection of British modern art.

Near the end of St John's Street, at the left-hand bend, bear right and then cross over Friary Lane into East Pallant car park. The trail bears left through the car park here and along South East Walls Walk into Cawley Priory car park. Cross over South Pallant and head along Theatre Lane to

Here, the trail turns right alongside the Avenue from where you can see the surviving Roman bastion and a well-preserved section of wall. Just before the roundabout at the junction with West Street, you can detour off right through the pedestrian entrance to the Bishop's Palace Gardens and explore this peaceful city park.

Continue over West Street and then head along North Walls. Accessible off West Street is the Novium Museum, whose exhibition spaces about Chichester's heritage are built over the remains of a Roman bathhouse. After 75m, fork left up onto North Walls Walk and follow the final section of raised path for just under 500m back to North Street, where a right turn will take you back to the Market Cross.

◀ Chichester Cathedral from the Bishop's Palace Gardens

Chidham Peninsula and Cobnor Point

Distance 8km **Time** 2 hours
Terrain fields and shoreline paths with one section inaccessible at high tide (tide times can be checked at www.conservancy.co.uk)
Map OS Explorer OL8 **Access** no public transport to the start

Take your binoculars for the handy bird hide on this route that loops around a coastal headland.

The walk starts from Cobnor Farm Amenity car park along Chidham Lane at the southern edge of Chidham village. Chidham Peninsula has been inhabited and farmed for more than 10,000 years. Today, there is a mixture of crop fields and marshland, with Nutbourne Marshes designated as a Local Nature Reserve. Located between Thorney Island and Bosham Peninsula, Chidham Peninsula lies alongside the waters of Chichester Harbour, whose saltmarshes and intertidal areas provide a haven for birdlife, in particular curlews, oystercatchers and redshank. It is also possible to spot harbour and grey seals swimming in the shallow waters or resting up on mudflats exposed at low tide. Please note, a section of this route to the west of Cobnor Point passes along the shingle foreshore which floods at high tide and is then temporarily inaccessible.

Head out of the rear of the car park and turn left onto the permissive path along the field edge to the path junction by Bosham Channel. The route turns right and follows the path alongside the tidal water's edge for the next 1km. The path then doglegs away from the shore past a pier and Cobnor Activities Centre before returning to the water's edge. From here, continue for 500m on a surfaced path over a couple of footbridges to Cobnor Point, where there are views over Chichester Channel to Itchenor

CHIDHAM PENINSULA AND COBNOR POINT

◂ Looking across Bosham Channel to the village of Bosham

and westwards to the Isle of Wight.

The path continues to circle round to the right and after another 300m reaches a set of steps down onto the foreshore. From here the path heads along the foreshore, which is covered and inaccessible either side of high tide. You soon pass a bird hide and after another 750m the footpath heads back up some steps onto the top of the tide bank and takes you over Nutbourne Marshes a little away from the foreshore. After just under 2km, the path comes alongside the foreshore again and in another 250m reaches a footpath junction.

Turn sharp right over a ditch here, double back along the field edge and follow it round to the left over three fields to Cot Lane. Turn right along the lane for a little under 100m and, just past Chedeham House, fork left onto a footpath along the right-hand field edge into the village of Chidham. Continue ahead down Cot Lane and round the right bend to St Mary's Church. Just beyond, turn sharp left onto a wide grassy footpath which after 350m bends left, crosses a ditch and continues along the field edge beyond. Before the end of the field, make sure you fork left at the marker post down to Chidham Lane and then bear right along the lane back to the car park at the start.

8 AROUND CHICHESTER

West Itchenor and Chichester Channel

Distance 5.75km **Time** 1 hour 30
Terrain tidal shoreline, lanes and fields
Map OS Explorer OL8 **Access** no public transport to the start

Enjoy the mix of coastal and countryside scenery on this short walk from a village at the mouth of Chichester Harbour.

The walk starts from the village of West Itchenor, which is situated off the road from Chichester to West Wittering on the south side of the Chichester Channel. Parking is available in Chichester Harbour Conservancy car park off The Street. The somewhat unusual name Itchenor comes from a Saxon chieftain called Icca and the Saxon word *ora*, a bank on the shore. The village is officially called West Itchenor, though the settlement of East Itchenor disappeared in the 15th century. During the 17th and 18th centuries, there was a considerable amount of ship-building and there are still some boatyards near the quay. The place is popular in summer with sailors who launch their boats from the quay and with visitors taking the ferry for a trip across to Bosham.

From the quay by the Harbour Office, which used to be a Custom House and is now home to Chichester Harbour Conservancy, walk down The Street and, opposite The Ship Inn, turn left onto a footpath along the entrance driveway to Itchenor Sailing Club. The footpath goes past the clubhouse and turns right alongside the water's edge past jetties and moorings. After 400m, the path bends right and then heads away from the shoreline to a gate onto Spinney Lane.

Turn left and head past the houses for 400m to the end of the lane, where the footpath heads off right through Westlands Copse. Continue across the field beyond to the far side, turn right

◀ The view across the Chichester Channel near West Itchenor

along the field edge and continue over the next field to Itchenor Road. The route turns right along the road past the village pond to the Church of St Nicholas, patron saint of seafarers. Inside the church are some interesting stained-glass memorial windows, among which, on the south wall of the nave, is one featuring St Christopher carrying a child, with a Swordfish aeroplane in a panel below, and St Nicholas of Bari carrying a sailboat.

Continue for 150m along the road past the church to the bend and take the footpath ahead up the farm road to Itchenor Park House and Farm. Bend right in front of the entrance to the house and head past the barns to a junction with a track. The footpath turns left along the track between fields for 800m to a gate. Fork slightly right here and continue along the edge of a field to a path junction by the Chichester Channel.

The final part of the walk turns right and follows the path by the shoreline for just over 1km, initially along a hedged section, then through an oakwood and finally over Chalkdock Marsh. There is a section of boardwalk here and the path can very occasionally become inundated at an exceptionally high tide (tide times can be checked at the Harbour Office).

The path now heads away from the water's edge and goes past a permissive path off right back to the car park, before heading through a boatyard and along the backs of gardens to the quay in West Itchenor.

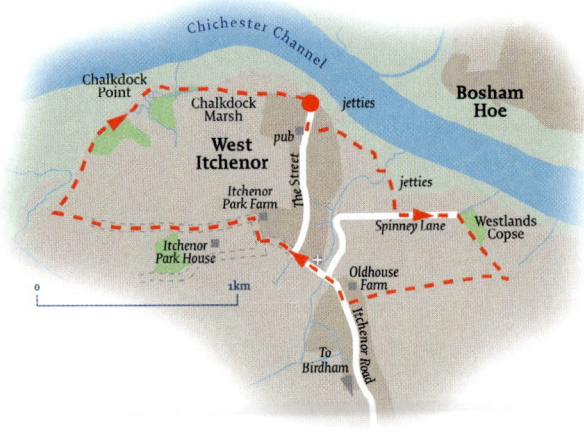

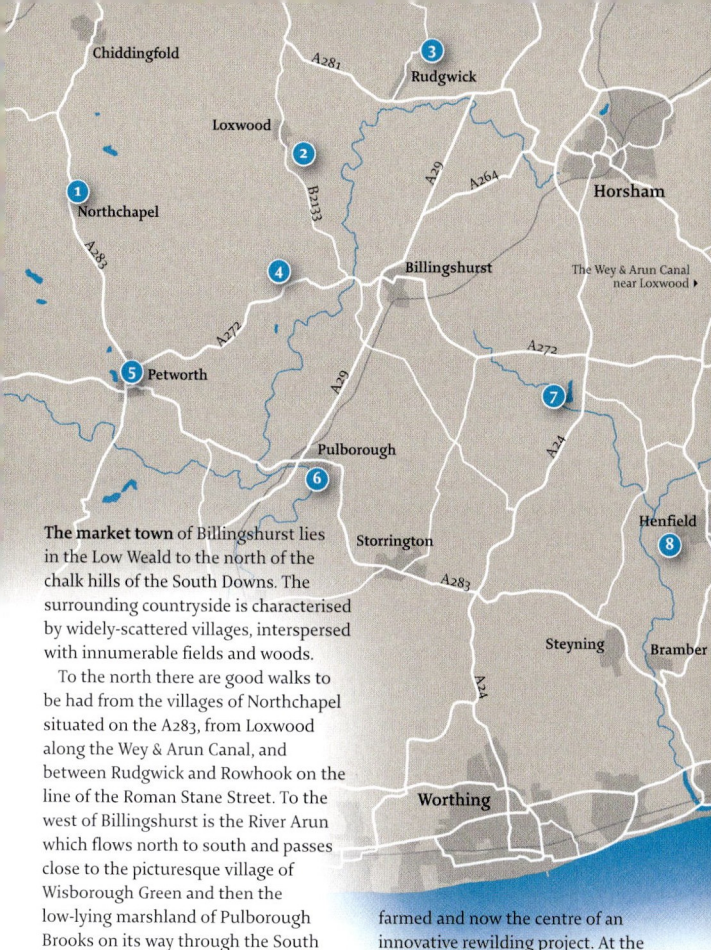

The Wey & Arun Canal near Loxwood ▶

The market town of Billinghurst lies in the Low Weald to the north of the chalk hills of the South Downs. The surrounding countryside is characterised by widely-scattered villages, interspersed with innumerable fields and woods.

To the north there are good walks to be had from the villages of Northchapel situated on the A283, from Loxwood along the Wey & Arun Canal, and between Rudgwick and Rowhook on the line of the Roman Stane Street. To the west of Billinghurst is the River Arun which flows north to south and passes close to the picturesque village of Wisborough Green and then the low-lying marshland of Pulborough Brooks on its way through the South Downs to the coast.

Southeast from Billinghurst and close to the busy dual-carriageways of the A24 is Knepp Castle Estate, once intensively farmed and now the centre of an innovative rewilding project. At the eastern limit of this central section lies the village of Henfield on the A281 and the upper reaches of another once busy tidal waterway, the River Adur.

Billingshurst and the Low Weald

1 Northchapel 44
Find peace and solitude on this countryside loop not far from busy Petworth

2 Loxwood and the Wey & Arun Canal 46
Combine this short walk with a summer cruise on board a narrowboat or a visit to the pub

3 Rudgwick and Rowhook 48
Follow the line of a Roman road and reflect on the area's much less orderly early resident, the giant armadillo-like *Horshamosaurus Rudgwickensis*

4 Wisborough Green 50
Visit on a summer weekend and combine this circuit with watching some village cricket

5 Petworth 52
This short walk will leave plenty of time to visit nearby Petworth House and Park

6 Pulborough Brooks 54
Art and wildlife lovers will find plenty to look at along this route over marshes

7 Knepp Castle Estate 56
This route takes you past the former home of the writer Hilaire Belloc, who considered Sussex his 'spiritual home'

8 Henfield and the River Adur 58
There's plenty of history on this route and you can find out more at Henfield Museum in the village centre

Northchapel

Distance 7km **Time** 2 hours
Terrain fields and woodland
Map OS Explorer OL33 **Access** bus to Northchapel from Midhurst

Stride out over fields and through woodland on this circuit in the heart of the Low Weald.

The walk starts from the village of Northchapel, 9km north of Petworth and close to the border with Surrey. Parking is available along Pipers Lane beside the village green or in the visitors' car park behind St Michael's Church. The church, tucked behind some houses, is Victorian but in the village there are many far older houses, some timber-framed and clad with brick and tile in local Sussex fashion, while others date from the Georgian and Victorian periods. The A283 runs north to south through the village and somewhat divides it, but there is still a large green, which marks the oldest part of the village.

Over the centuries, the surrounding fields and woods of the Low Weald supported many of the village's trades and industries, such as ironworking, glassmaking, quarrying, coppicing and brickmaking.

From the A283 just to the north of St Michael's Church, walk along Pipers Lane for 250m past the large village green and take the bridleway off left just before the village hall. The bridleway heads along a track past cottages and then up the left edge of two fields into Frith Wood. Here, bear right for 200m to a staggered bridleway crosspaths. Make a short dogleg right, then left to continue along the bridleway down the driveway to Frith Hill Court.

Just past the house, fork right onto the bridleway which heads gently down between fields through The Plantation. After 750m, look out for a fingerpost and footpath off right through a gate into

The Old Forge in Northchapel

fields. Walk along the edge of two fields, bear right along a track to Mitchell Park Farm and pass in front of the farmhouse. Keep ahead down the small field beyond, across the head of a pond and up steps to Pipers Lane. The route crosses the lane and continues on a track along the edge of three more fields, where you can see an air navigational beacon over to the right. At the end of the third field, turn right for 100m along the edge of the next field to a marker post. Go left through the gap in the hedge and turn right, heading down across a small stream in woodland to a stile back into fields.

Follow the waymarks up the left side of the field beyond to a gate, turn left over the rise of the next field and head past the cowsheds of Freehold Farm to its driveway. Bear right with the footpath along the driveway, which soon bends right by some barns. Follow the driveway for another 600m past the Scots pines of Mercers Furze plantation, past a stand of poplar trees and then down through a narrow section of deciduous woodland to a bridleway crosspaths.

Leave the driveway here and turn right onto the bridleway, which heads gently uphill for just over 1km through woodland, over a bridleway crosspaths and then along the edge of the wood. At the far side of the wood, bend right with the track up to Hortons Farm, where a left turn will take you back along Pipers Lane to the start.

Loxwood and the Wey & Arun Canal

Distance 5.75km **Time** 1 hour 30
Terrain towpath, lanes and woodland paths **Map** OS Explorer OL34
Access bus to Loxwood from Horsham and Pulborough (very limited service)

Meander beside the tranquil waters of a restored canal before circling back through woodland.

The walk starts from Loxwood, where parking is available in the Wey & Arun Canal Trust car park, which lies beyond the Onslow Arms and its own car park for customers. The Canal Trust car park is popular and can become full at busy periods. From the High Street, the B2133, at the southern end of Loxwood, walk along the canal towpath past The Onslow Arms and the Wey & Arun Canal Trust Centre on the Wey-South Path, which is followed for the first half of the walk.

The Wey & Arun Canal was completed in 1816 and linked the Wey Navigation near Guildford in Surrey with the south coast via the Arun Navigation, with the intention of creating a supply route between London and Portsmouth. Barges imported groceries, coal, provisions and even seaweed for use as fertiliser, while carrying away timber, flour and farm produce. However, the growing railway network provided cheaper and faster transport and after just 50 years the canal fell into disrepair and closed. It remained abandoned for a century until the formation of the Wey & Arun Canal Society in 1970. Today the 37km waterway is undergoing restoration and has become popular not only with narrowboat enthusiasts but also with walkers, cyclists and horseriders. On this section of the canal, there are even scheduled cruises during the summer months aboard an electrically-powered narrowboat.

The Wey & Arun Canal near Baldwin's Knob Lock

The towpath beside the canal is wide and makes for pleasant walking as it meanders its way for 2.5km past the restored canal's locks and bridges to Drungewick Aqueduct, and, just beyond, Drungewick Lane. Here, continue along the Wey-South Path which turns right, heading gently up the tree-lined lane.

After 600m, by Bumble Farm, leave the Wey-South Path and turn right onto the bridleway that leads down the driveway past the farmhouse and into woodland. The pleasant tree-fringed bridleway rises gently between fields up to Hooklane Copse. Bear left with the bridleway here to soon join a wide forestry track. After another 150m, as the track curves right, look out for a fingerpost marking a crosspaths.

Turn right onto the footpath which heads gently down through the wood beside a fence for 200m and then bends a little to the left and drops more steeply down beside a streambed to a footbridge. Cross the bridge and continue on the far side for 50m to a junction with a forestry path. Turn left over the rise through Birch Copse down to a gate. The footpath continues ahead along a fenced section and soon bends left between fields to a track. Turn right down the track for 250m to Brewhurst Lane, which carries a bridleway. A right turn onto the bridleway takes you down to the former Brewhurst Mill, where a footpath leads off left over a couple of footbridges and then a meadow back to the canal. Turn left back along the towpath to return to the start.

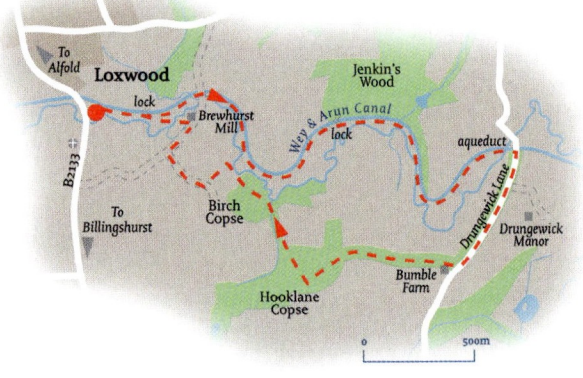

BILLINGSHURST AND THE LOW WEALD

Rudgwick and Rowhook

Distance 9km **Time** 2 hours 30
Terrain fields and woods
Map OS Explorer OL34 **Access** bus to Rudgwick from Guildford, Cranleigh and Horsham

Follow ancient paths and tracks over farmland, through woods and along a short stretch of Roman road.

The walk starts from the village of Rudgwick (pronounced Ridgick), where roadside parking is available on the B2128. The name means 'farm on a hill' and the ridge, on which the church and original part of the village stand, used to mark the boundary between Surrey and Sussex. Somewhat further back in time, the area was home to a unique armoured dinosaur species, known as *Horshamosaurus Rudgwickensis* after the Rudgwick quarry where its fossils were found.

Walk up the pavement of the B2128 to the northern end of the village and take the footpath off right by The King's Head past Holy Trinity Church, which houses a Romanesque font made from Sussex marble. Continue through the graveyard and over a field to Highcroft Drive. Bear left past a house, beyond which a footpath continues between fields to a junction with a driveway.

Turn left onto the driveway, which carries a bridleway, for just over 500m to the entrance driveway to Hermongers. Here, continue ahead onto a footpath between fields to a track, with a view left to the ridgeline of the Surrey Hills. Bear left with the footpath along the track, which winds its way between fields for the next 800m to Bury St Austen's Farm. By the entrance to the farmhouse, continue ahead past the farm buildings, before continuing along the track for another 1km up to Ridge Farm.

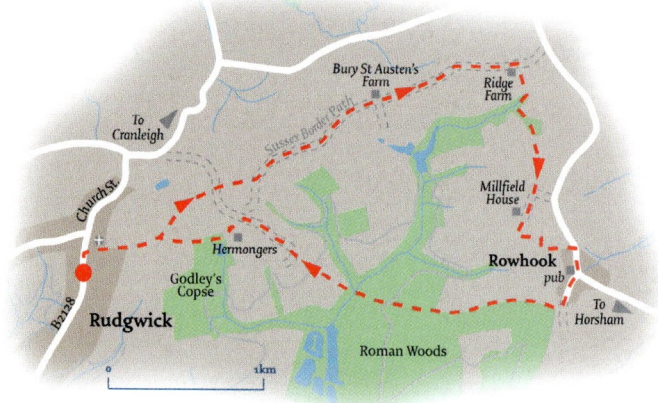

At the far end of the buildings turn right onto a footpath which heads down a track to the bottom of the field beyond. Here, dogleg briefly right to a marker post, then left into the narrow wood. The footpath now crosses two footbridges, bends to the left and continues gently up through the strip of trees – if the path is overgrown here, use one of the field edges to left or right. At the end of the trees, keep ahead along the edge of the field beyond. After 150m, look out for a gap in the hedge where a fingerpost shows the way ahead alongside a fence and then up a tree-lined path to the driveway to Millfield House. Follow the driveway for 150m and, at the bend, keep ahead into fields. Follow the footpath along the left-hand edge of the first field, and then turn left along the right-hand edges of the next two fields to Rowhook Road. Turn right into Rowhook to the junction with Waterlands Lane by The Chequers Inn.

The onward route turns right up Waterlands Lane for 250m along the line of what was Stane Street, the Roman road between Noviomagus Reginorum (Chichester) and Londinium. At the top of the rise, take the bridleway off right down past timber-framed Burnt House into woodland. The bridleway, which can be muddy, heads westwards for the next 1.3km down through Roman Woods to a footbridge. At the bridleway junction beyond, keep ahead uphill out of the wood and continue up the left field edge to a track. Follow this for 400m past the houses and turn left by the entrance to Hermongers House onto a footpath which leads down a driveway past old stables into Street Copse. Continue along the footpath up through the trees and over a field. At the far side, cross the driveway and retrace your steps to the start.

◀ Fields near Bury St Austen's Farm

Wisborough Green

Distance 9km **Time** 2 hours 15
Terrain lanes, fields and canal-side path
Map OS Explorer OL34 **Access** bus to
Wisborough Green from Horsham,
Billingshurst and Pulborough
(limited service)

This walk over fields and alongside a canal and a river is short enough to leave plenty of time to explore a gem of a Sussex village.

Wisborough Green has the appearance of a quintessential English village with a large green on which cricket is played, a pond and a church on raised ground, while to its east lies the River Arun and low-lying fields. The name of the village originates from the Anglo-Saxon *wisc beorg*, which has the suitable meaning 'hill by the river meadow'.

From the centre of Wisborough Green at the southern end of the cricket ground, walk down the pavement of Billingshurst Road, the A272, for 100m. Turn left along School Road past the pond and bear right up the walkway to the Church of St Peter ad Vincula. The chancel contains some medieval wall paintings, rediscovered in the 19th century, and in the south aisle is a memorial window to the Huguenot glassworkers who fled here from France in the 16th century during the Wars of Religion. The north aisle houses the delightful Wisborough Tapestry, a 20th-century work by local residents which depicts aspects of village life and history.

Continue past the church, down through the graveyard and along the path to Glebe Way and its junction with the A272. Cross over and follow the bridleway opposite for the next 1km down an undulating lane to Harsfold Farmhouse. Keep ahead with the bridleway along a track down between fields and through a

WISBOROUGH GREEN

◀ In Wisborough Green

gate to a bridge over the River Arun. Continue for another 150m to the bridge over the Wey & Arun Canal.

A left turn now takes you onto the route of the Wey-South Path, which is followed for the middle part of the walk. This heads alongside the canal and after 700m crosses Flood Gate Bridge to continue on the far side. It then passes over three further footbridges to Lording's Lock, where there is a waterwheel and a picnic table. The Wey-South Path continues over fields – head up the narrow field on the left and then follow the left field edge alongside the line of the canal, which is now filled in here. At the far end of the field, the path turns left through a section of woodland between the canal and the River Arun. After 250m, you bend back right and head along field edges, with the River Arun off to the right, to a footbridge near the site of Guildenhurst Bridge. Cross the footbridge and continue ahead for another 300m to the A272 at New Bridge.

A little care is needed to cross the road here before continuing for another 1.2km between the river and a wide section of canal, past Northlands Lift Bridge, to a bridleway junction at Rowner Lock and Bridge. Leave the Wey-South Path here and turn left over the bridge onto the bridleway which heads up the right-hand edge of a field and then a track to Paplands Farm. Continue up Paplands Lane and cross over the B2133. The final part of the walk heads past The Bat and Ball pub along Newpound Lane, which twists its way for just over 1.5km back to the northern end of the cricket ground in Wisborough Green.

Petworth

Distance 5km **Time** 1 hour 30
Terrain lanes, steep-sided fields and woods **Map** OS Explorer OL33
Access bus to Petworth from Midhurst and Worthing

Escape the bustle of Petworth on this short but hilly walk to a neighbouring estate village.

Many visitors come to the estate town of Petworth for a tour of Petworth House, one of Southern England's best known mansions, and its extensive deer park. However, there is also plenty to see in and around the small estate town, especially the narrow streets around Market Square and Lombard Street. The small Petworth Cottage Museum on the High Street is the former home of a seamstress who worked at Petworth and has been restored to show how it would have looked in the early 20th century. This route explores the Leconfield Estate, Petworth's working estate, which lies across the steep-sided valley to the east.

From the top end of Petworth on North Street opposite St Mary's Church and the war memorial, head along Barton Lane and bend left down to a double gate at a crosspaths, where the view across the Shimmings Valley to the high ground of Brinksole Heath is dramatic. Head down the field ahead to the bottom of the valley and across the bridge over a stream. Climb up the far side to a gate and continue to the top of the brow. The footpath bears a little left here past the left-hand of two clumps of trees down to a swing gate. You now head up a wooded sunken path to a track junction at the edge of Brinksole Heath.

A right turn along the track takes you along the edge of the tree-covered heath for 250m to a triangle of tracks. Keep

◂ On Lombard Street in Petworth looking towards St Mary's Church

ahead for another 75m and turn sharp right with the public footpath to reach the fence in front of Goanah Lodges. Turn left here and descend the track out of the woodland and down to some barns on your left just before a bend in the track. At the bend, the footpath leaves the track and goes straight on through a gate along a fenced section between fields down to the A283 – since being fenced this section is prone to being a little overgrown, depending on whether the farmer has had time to mow it. At the road, a little care is needed to dogleg right for 50m along the narrow pavement and then left across the road back into fields. Aim to the left of the house visible on the far side to a stile in the field's bottom left corner, which leads down to a lane. Turn right through the estate village of Byworth, round the right bend and past The Black Horse Inn.

Just before the junction with the A283, take the footpath off left down beside a field, then more steeply down through woodland and over a footbridge to a path junction. Here, turn right out of the wood and then fork left steeply up the rough field beyond to a crosspaths by houses. Keep ahead and follow the path up along the field edge and past the allotments to Grove Street.

A right turn here will take you in 500m past Petworth Cottage Museum on the High Street to Market Square, from where narrow cobbled Lombard Street heads back up to the church.

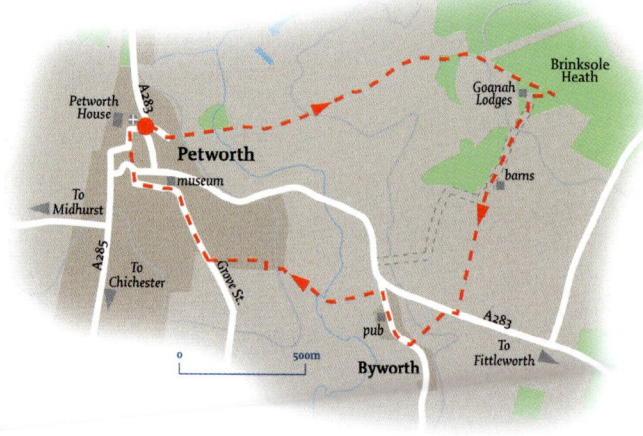

Pulborough Brooks

Distance 6km (including detour to RSPB visitor centre) **Time** 1 hour 30 **Terrain** fields and marshland (can be muddy and prone to flooding) **Map** OS Explorer OL10 **Access** bus to Pulborough from Burgess Hill, Billingshurst and Horsham; trains to Pulborough Station (1km from the start along the WildArt Trail) from Arundel and Horsham

Stride out over one of Sussex's most extensive natural wetlands with the option to call in at its RSPB visitor centre.

The walk starts from Lower Street, the A283, in Pulborough near its junction with Brooks Way, where there is a car park. An alternative would be to start halfway along the route at Pulborough Brooks RSPB Visitor Centre, which has a car park. The first half of the walk also follows part of the Pulborough WildArt Trail, a series of sculptures and digital works by Sussex-based artist Steve Geliot.

From Lower Street take the footpath, signed for the RSPB Pulborough Brooks Nature Reserve, down narrow Barn House Lane past the rear entrance to the car park and cottages to a gate onto the marshland. The path descends across a ditch, heads alongside another ditch and then forks left to soon see a footbridge. Cross the footbridge and continue alongside the River Arun to a gate by a ditch. Here, you are crossing the line of the Roman causeway which connected Stane Street, which lies to the west of the Brooks, with the Roman fort and settlement at Pevensey. The footpath continues for another 200m beside the river before bending left to a gate into the RSPB nature reserve.

Follow the public footpath up a track and over a crosspaths to a field gate. From

PULBOROUGH BROOKS

◀ Wiggonholt Church

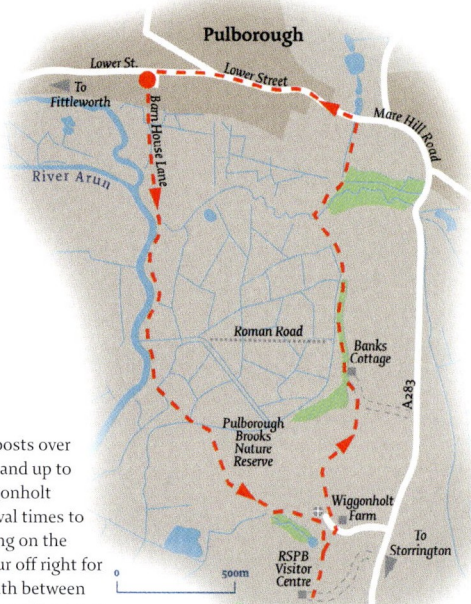

here, follow the fingerposts over two fields, across a dip and up to the lane past tiny Wiggonholt Church, built in medieval times to serve shepherds working on the marshes. You can detour off right for 350m down a fenced path between fields and up through woodland to the RSPB visitor centre, which has information on the reserve and a café.

The onward route crosses the lane beyond Wiggonholt Church by the entrance to the Old Rectory and bends left into fields. Follow the footpath fingerposts over three fields down to a track. Descend the track for 100m to the bend and look out for the footpath sign taking you off left on a path down onto the marshland below Banks Cottage.

The footpath now tracks its way northwards for the next 750m along the eastern side of the marsh, where it passes over the route of the Roman causeway just past Banks Cottage and then over two stiles, before edging along a field to a footbridge over a ditch. Cross the footbridge, turn right along the ditch for 150m and then bear left to a stile by a field gate at the edge of the marsh. Head up the tree-lined path beyond and then a track to Mare Hill Road, the A283. From here, turn left onto the path along the grassy verge and then follow the pavement up round the left bend into Lower Street for the final 750m back to the start.

Knepp Castle Estate

Distance 10km **Time** 2 hours 30
Terrain fields, parkland and woods
Maps OS Explorer OL10 and OL34
Access no public transport to the start

Experience one of Europe's most ambitious rewilding projects on this waymarked route.

Knepp Estate was first owned by Sussex iron-masters in the 16th to 18th centuries and its parkland later landscaped by Humphry Repton and adorned with a mansion designed by John Nash. Its fields were farmed increasingly intensively in the last century, but today the estate is home to a remarkable conservation project, creating a biodiverse wilderness in the Low Weald of Sussex.

The walk starts from the Knepp Estate Walkers car park, which is accessed from Worthing Road, the A24 access road, near the village of Dial Post. At the far end of the car park is Knepp Wilding Kitchen and Shop, which has a café and public toilets. The route follows the Knepp Estate's waymarked Red Walk.

Head back out of the entrance of the car park and follow signs across a field to Swallows Lane. Cross the lane, go through the gate by the cattle grid and along the wooded track for 50m. The Red Walk turns left here onto a permissive path and then a footpath across a series of five fields to a bridleway junction by Wickwood Cottage. The route now turns right along Bentons Lane, which can be muddy, and after 400m bends right to a gate. In front of the gate, fork right off the bridleway and follow the waymarks over two fields, beyond which you bend left over Lancing Brook and along the edge of a third field to a junction with a track. Here, you can make a detour off right for 300m to a treehouse viewing platform alongside an old canal which used to connect to the River Adur.

The onward route forks left along the

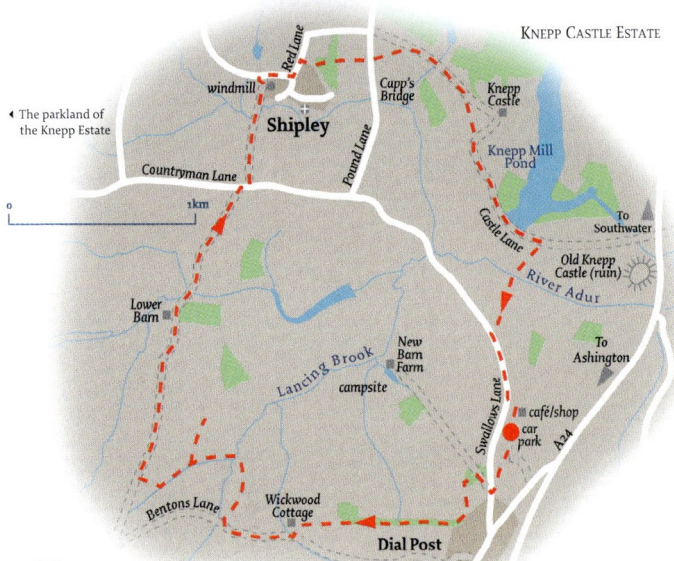

◀ The parkland of the Knepp Estate

track for 350m to a bridleway crosspaths. Turn right here along the tree-lined bridleway for the next 1.7km past another treehouse viewing platform and then Lower Barn to reach Countryman Lane. A short dogleg right, then left takes you onto a bridleway along the bed of the old canal and across a couple of footbridges to King's Land and School Lane in Shipley. The house and windmill here were once owned by the writer Hilaire Belloc, who lived in the village for almost 50 years until his death in 1953. Turn right along School Lane to the junction with Red Lane, where you can detour off right to the church. The composer John Ireland is buried here and there is also a commemorative plaque inside the church.

At the junction, bend left along Red Lane and, just beyond the last house, turn right and head over fields and through woodland, before crossing Pound Lane and the parkland beyond to the driveway to Knepp Castle. From here, turn right up the 19th-century mansion's driveway for 250m, fork right over the grass to Castle Lane and follow it for 500m down to Knepp Mill Pond, where an information panel explains its history.

The final part of the route continues across the head of the pond and then turns sharp right onto a bridleway down across a footbridge over the River Adur, with a view to the medieval ruins of Old Knepp Castle, and up fields to Swallows Lane. Go left along the lane and, after the turning for Swallows Farm, turn left off the lane to cross through the courtyard of Knepp Wilding Kitchen to the car park.

Henfield and the River Adur

Distance 7.5km **Time** 2 hours
Terrain old lanes, riverside path and former railway line **Map** OS Explorer OL11
Access bus from Henfield village centre and Worthing stops on Station Road near the start of the route

A varied countryside walk takes you alongside the River Adur, once a busy tidal waterway.

The walks starts from the car park on Upper Station Road where the Downs Link path crosses, 1km to the west of the centre of the large village of Henfield. Part of the route follows the Downs Link, along which the Horsham to Shoreham Railway ran from 1861 to 1966. In addition to passengers, the railway was used to provide regular deliveries of fruit, vegetables and flowers, including the famous Henfield Violets, to London markets. The Henfield Violet Nurseries was a pioneering Edwardian business, founded in 1900 by Ada Brown and Decima Allen. They were members of the Royal Horticultural Society and, with connections to members of the Bloomsbury Group, were also active in the women's suffrage movement.

From the car park, follow the signs for the Downs Link across Upper Station Road and down Station Road to the bend. Turn right along Hollands Lane and, where the Downs Link heads off left, continue ahead past buildings and then down the bridleway track, signed for Rye House. The route now continues for a little over 1.5km along Hollands Lane, which is periodically surfaced, between fields and past Canons and Leeches, former yeoman farmers' houses, down to New Inn Farm, which served as both a farm and an inn until the early 20th century. Continue ahead along the bridleway, which passes to the right of the farm buildings and across a field to

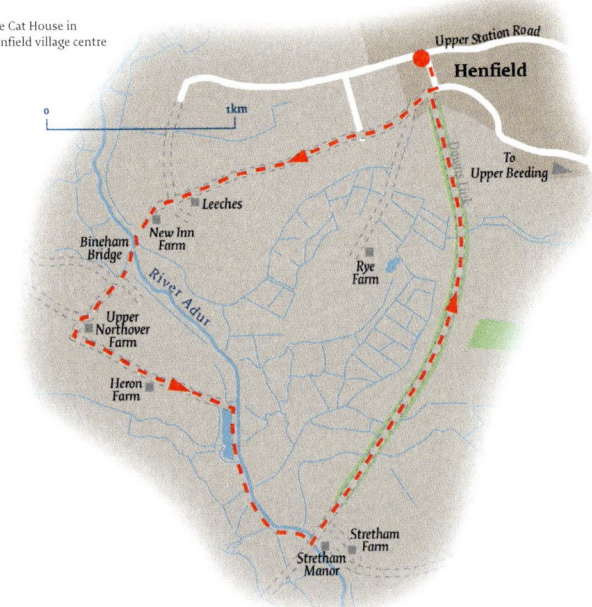

◀ The Cat House in Henfield village centre

Bineham Bridge over the River Adur. The river here is tidal and in the 19th century transported goods such as coal, chalk, timber and malt on long barges.

The route crosses the bridge and continues along the bridleway past the Malt House up to a track junction by Upper Northover Farm. Turn left and follow the track for the next 1km round the left bend and past Heron Farm back to the River Adur. Turn right and follow the bridleway for 1km along the bank of the River Adur to the junction with the Downs Link path at the bridge by Stretham Manor. Stretham Manor was the first settled part of Henfield parish – *Stret* gives an etymological clue that the house is located on the line of a now lost Roman road, which crossed the River Adur here and enabled trade from Chichester to London. For the final part of the walk, turn left for just over 2.5km of easy walking on the tree-lined Downs Link path to the junction with Hollands Lane, where you turn right and then retrace your steps up Station Road to the start.

Arundel Castle from the banks of the River Arun ▶

The medieval town of Arundel with its prominent castle and cathedral presents an imposing view when seen from the south along the A27 and attracts crowds of visitors. Walkers are drawn to the slopes of the downs which lie to the northwest of the town and their high points on Glatting Beacon and Bignor Hill, over which marches Roman Stane Street on its way from Chichester past the famous Roman villa at Bignor to London.

The hill on which Arundel is built overlooks the River Arun, which flows southwards past Amberley and through a gap carved in the South Downs before passing below the town on its way to the coast by Littlehampton. On the valley's eastern side opposite Arundel stands the little village of Burpham, once a Saxon stronghold against Viking incursions and now a good setting-off point into the rolling downland that stretches eastwards above Littlehampton and Worthing.

The northern escarpment of these hills rises to Kithurst Hill, easily accessed from the small town of Storrington, and extends all the way to Annington Hill before dipping down to the broad valley of the River Adur by the village of Bramber at the eastern limit of this section. The coast to the south of the downs is largely one long strip of conurbation, with the delightful exception of Climping Beach, just to the west of Littlehampton.

Around Arundel and Worthing

1 Glatting Beacon and Bignor Hill 62
This route passes close to Bignor Roman Villa, famous for some of the finest mosaics in Britain

2 Slindon Park and Estate 64
Wander around the park and village lanes where the writer Hilaire Belloc lived as a boy and young man

3 Climping Beach 66
A pair of binoculars will be useful for some seabird-spotting, but watch out also for flying golf balls

4 Amberley 68
Take the train and you can easily combine this walk with a visit to Amberley Museum

5 Arundel and Swanbourne Lake 70
Come for the day and experience all the sights that this historic town has on offer

6 Burpham 72
Look out for the village's Saxon burgh, once a stronghold against raiding Vikings

7 Storrington and Kithurst Hill 74
Enjoy a short but challenging route from a bustling village on the edge of the South Downs

8 Bramber and Annington Hill 76
Explore a castle, a church and a former inn once you've taken in the view from the top of the downs

Glatting Beacon and Bignor Hill

Distance 8.5km **Time** 2 hours 30
Terrain lanes, woodland and fields, open
downland **Map** OS Explorer OL10
Access bus to Sutton from Petworth and
Chichester (flexible request service, 99
Flex from compass-travel.co.uk)

**Climb steeply up a wooded escarpment
and follow downland tracks in use since
before the Romans came.**

The walk starts from the secluded village of Sutton, which lies below the northern edge of the downs near Bignor and its famous Roman villa. From the junction in the middle of the village by the bus stop and the White Horse Inn, walk up the lane signed for Barlavington and Duncton for 750m past houses, over the rise and down to a junction at the bend. Fork left here down the no-through-way wooded lane for 250m and at the left-hand bend take the bridleway off right.

This initially heads along a track – which can be wet if the small stream is flowing down its length – and then climbs uphill, steeply at times, along a sunken path between high banks lined with beech and yew up to a bridleway junction near the top of the wood. Continue ahead and follow the bridleway round to the left for just under 500m up a track to a field gate, with the radio masts on Glatting Beacon visible ahead. Keep ahead up the field to a second gate into the National Trust land of Bignor Hill, from where there is a good view back over the high ground of Littleton Down. Follow the bridleway ahead along the track through the woodland below the masts on Glatting Beacon and continue downhill, past the junction with the South Downs Way, to the car park at

GLATTING BEACON AND BIGNOR HILL

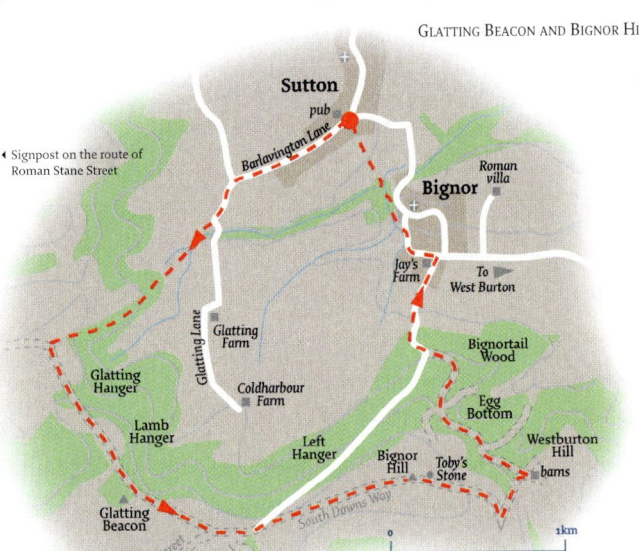

◀ Signpost on the route of Roman Stane Street

the top of the lane up from Bignor, near where the Roman road Stane Street crosses (the raised bank is still visible).

The onward route follows the South Downs Way along a flint-cobbled track up to the top of Bignor Hill, where you pass the memorial of Toby's Stone. Continue down the South Downs Way which, after 400m, zigzags steeply down to a five-way junction by some hay barns in the dip below Westburton Hill. Turn sharp left here onto a track, which carries a bridleway, back uphill.

After 250m, the track bends right, heads over the rise and then descends gently through woodland round the steep-sided combe above Egg Bottom. After the track bends round to the north, you cross over a track junction and then descend more steeply down to the lane up from Bignor.

The route now turns right down the steep lane for 600m to the junction by Jay's Farm – initially the lane descends between high banks and, to avoid any traffic, you can follow the parallel path along the top of the steep wooded bank on the right and rejoin the lane lower down. At Jay's Farm, turn left up the narrow lane, go round the bend past Malthouse Cottages and take the next footpath off left down into woodland. The path descends into a dell and then crosses a series of three footbridges to a field gate. The final part of the walk now heads uphill over three fields and between gardens back into Sutton.

Slindon Park and Estate

Distance 3.25km **Time** 50 minutes
Terrain woodland paths and village lanes
Map OS Explorer OL10 **Access** bus to Slindon from Amberley, Storrington and Chichester (very limited service)

Follow a waymarked trail around the pale of a medieval deer park and through a tranquil estate village.

The walk starts from the Slindon Estate National Trust car park on Park Lane on the southern edge of Slindon village. The National Trust, which manages the estate, has waymarked a walk (pink arrows) which follows Slindon Park's pale, a bank and ditch which was constructed in medieval times to keep deer in the park. Slindon House is in origin an Elizabethan mansion and is now a school. Many of the houses in the village belong to the estate and can be identified by their dark red paintwork.

The village also has two churches, one Anglican, St Mary's, and one Catholic, St Richard's. Slindon has a long history of Catholicism and St Richard's was completed in 1865 with money left in the will of the Earl of Newburgh, landowner of the Slindon Estate. One regular visitor to St Richard's soon after it was built was the future writer Hilaire Belloc. He came to live in Slindon as a boy in 1878 and lived in a number of houses in the village, including Bleak House on Top Road beyond the junction with Dyers Lane, before moving to Shipley in 1907.

From the rear of the car park, take the path off to the left into woodland for 100m to a crosspaths. Here, the trail turns left and heads through the trees and then alongside the park pale for 150m to a track junction. You now turn right and follow the track alongside the park pale on the southern edge of Slindon Park and then

Slindon Park and Estate

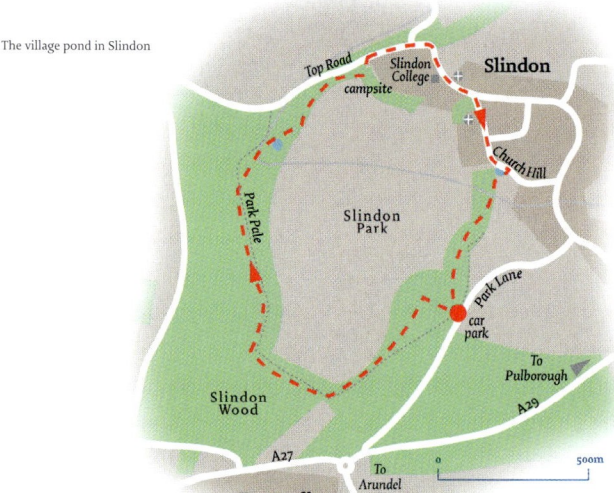

◀ The village pond in Slindon

round a right bend gently uphill for just over 500m along the park's western edge. The trail bends right and crosses through the pale and heads more steadily uphill, through a gate and then alongside a field, where you pass a handy walled bench, all that remains of an 18th-century tearoom. Continue up to the track junction by the entrance to Slindon campsite and bear left down the entrance track to the road.

The trail continues to the right on the path parallel to the road for 200m uphill through trees and then turns right along Top Road past the entrance to Slindon House, now occupied by Slindon College, and then St Richard's Catholic Church. Continue along the road to the junction and fork right down Church Hill past St Mary's Church, which contains a plaque commemorating Stephen Langton, Archbishop of Canterbury, who died in 1228 at Slindon Manor, a rare wooden effigy of Sir Anthony St Leger who died in 1539 and the David Beaty Memorial Window, engraved by Simon Whistler, son of Sir Lawrence Whistler. At the bottom of the hill, follow the road round to the left and just past the village pond look out for a marker post showing the way off right past the pond back into the trees. The trail forks left here and then heads gently downhill through the wood. After 300m, at a path junction, ignore the trail-marker indicating a right turn and keep ahead back down to the car park.

AROUND ARUNDEL AND WORTHING

Climping Beach

Distance 3.75km **Time** 1 hour
Terrain paths around a golf course and along a shingle beach
Map OS Explorer OL10 **Access** train to Littlehampton from Chichester and Worthing, accessible across Littlehampton Harbour Bridge, 700m from the route

Enjoy the quieter side of Littlehampton on this coastal circuit beside a tidal river, around the edge of a golf course and back over a shoreline nature reserve.

The walk starts from Littlehampton's West Beach car park, which is accessible by car along Ferry Road and Rope Walk off the A259, 1km west of the town. West Beach is separated from Littlehampton by the tidal and fast-flowing River Arun and is part of a wider area of shoreline referred to as Climping Beach. In 1993, West Beach was designated a Local Nature Reserve, while the whole of Climping Beach is a Site of Special Scientific Interest. The banks of the tidal river, the sandflats, dunes and shingle provide a haven for a wide variety of birds, plants and insects. You can spot oystercatchers, sandpipers and turnstones feeding on the flats exposed at low tide, sea kale and yellow horned poppy thrive on the banks of shingle above the high tide mark, and the dunes support more than 50 species of insect. In summer, ringed plovers nest on the high shingle and meadow pipits in the dunes, while in winter sanderlings heading south from the Arctic find rich pickings here in the zone between high and low tides.

From the car park, walk back up the entrance road past the Littlehampton Golf Course clubhouse and Arun Yacht Club, where you can fork right onto the footpath parallel with the road, past

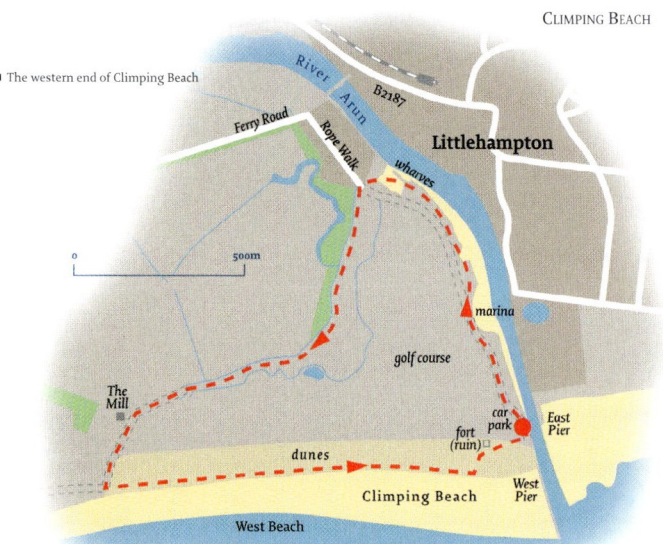

◀ The western end of Climping Beach

moorings and a marina beside the tidal waters of the River Arun. At the top of the entrance road, cross over onto a footpath which immediately heads past a tee of the golf course – before crossing in front of the tee, it's worth checking carefully to your right to make sure no one is teeing off.

The footpath passes along the edge of the course with woodland on the right for 500m and then bends right on a narrower path for another 600m to a footpath junction near the western end of the golf course. Fork left alongside a fence past The Mill – this section can be a little overgrown so a stick may come in handy. At the far side of the golf course, keep ahead to the start of the beach and the junction with the England Coast Path.

Depending on the state of the tide, you can now choose whether to turn immediately left onto the designated path along the shingle and grass at the top of the beach or head down below the high tide line. The distance to the West Pier at Littlehampton can seem further than the 1.3km it is, but it's worth taking your time and savouring this isolated stretch of beach on a coastline that is otherwise heavily built up. As you approach the pier, you'll need to bear left to the top of the beach and follow the path up over the dunes and along the boardwalks past the remains of Littlehampton Fort, a 19th-century artillery battery now largely covered by the shifting sands, to return to the car park at West Beach.

Amberley

Distance 5.5km **Time** 1 hour 30
Terrain lanes, marshland and riverside path (prone to flooding)
Map OS Explorer OL10 **Access** train to Amberley from Chichester and Horsham

This varied stroll wanders through one of Sussex's best-preserved villages in a real rural idyll.

The walk starts from Amberley Railway Station, which is located 1.5km south of Amberley village. There is parking available by the station and also along the route in Amberley itself at the village car park on School Road.

From the railway station, head down past the entrance to Amberley Museum, which contains exhibits about the area's rural and industrial past. Cross over the B2139, turn right and follow the walkway, and then the pavement, round the left bend and up the hill to the junction with High Titten. Cross back over the road and ready yourself for a fairly steep climb up High Titten lane for 600m to the junction by the entrance to Highdown. Turn left here down Mill Lane to the junction with the B2139 and cross over onto School Road. Head past the village car park and the school into Amberley village and take the first left into Church Street.

It's worth taking time to explore the village, where you'll find a tearoom, village stores, the Black Horse pub and a seemingly endless number of timber-framed and thatched houses.

Continue along Church Street past houses and cottages to St Michael's Church, which contains some medieval wall paintings and a memorial window to Edward Stott, an English painter of the late-Victorian to early 20th-century period and a member of the New English Art Club. In the mid-1880s he settled

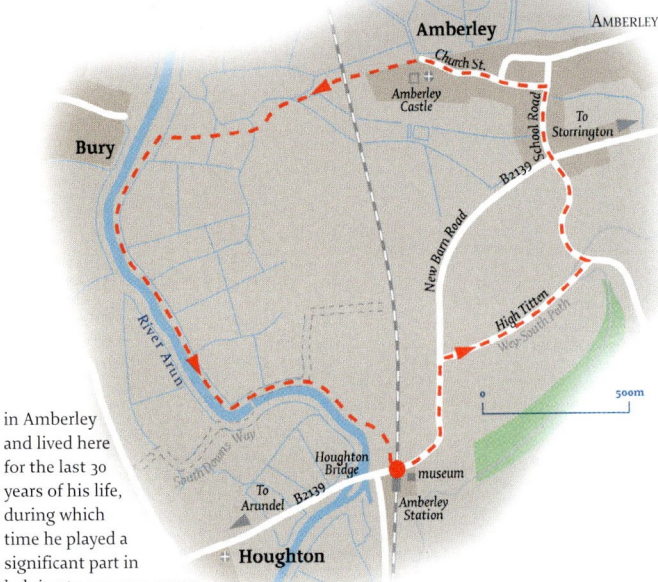

in Amberley and lived here for the last 30 years of his life, during which time he played a significant part in helping to preserve many of the thatched cottages. He was drawn to French plein air painting and the Impressionists and his own paintings of rural life and the surrounding Sussex landscapes achieved considerable success in his lifetime. In the churchyard, on its east side, there is a further memorial to Edward Stott by the sculptor Francis Derwent Wood. In addition, on the west wall of the churchyard is a tablet in memory of Arthur Rackham, the artist and illustrator, who lived in the village during the 1930s.

The route heads down past the church and forks left onto a footpath alongside the wall of the ruined castle, in origin a 900-year-old fortified manor house and now a hotel. Continue ahead over the railway line and the low-lying fields beyond for 700m to the footpath junction on the raised bank near the River Arun, across which until the 1950s a small ferry served the village of Bury opposite. The route now turns left and takes you along the footpath on the raised bank parallel to and then alongside the river to a sharp left bend. Follow the path round the bend, through a gate and past the footbridge which carries the South Downs Way. Keep ahead past the junction where the South Downs Way turns off left and follow the riverside path for another 250m before bearing left past chalets to the B2139 at Houghton Bridge. Here, a left turn will take you under the railway bridge back to the entrance to Amberley Station.

◀ The northern wall of Amberley Castle

Arundel and Swanbourne Lake

Distance 6.5km **Time** 1 hour 45
Terrain river, lake and parkland paths
Map OS Explorer OL10 **Access** bus to Arundel from Chichester and Worthing; train to Arundel from Horsham and Bognor Regis

This loop beside the River Arun and back through parkland gives wonderful views over the market town of Arundel.

The town is dominated by its castle, cathedral and river. The walls and towers of the home of the Dukes of Norfolk have occupied the hill above the town since the 12th century. Just as spectacular and imposing on the hill's western side is the Victorian Catholic cathedral, built in French Gothic style and commissioned by the 15th Duke of Norfolk. The River Arun flows past the town to the south and the east, while to the north lie Arundel Park and the Downs.

The walk starts from the bottom of the High Street in Arundel at the junction with Queen Street and Mill Road, opposite the entrance to Arundel Castle and Gardens. Take the riverside path that heads past the site of Blackfriars Priory and behind Arundel Museum. The footpath keeps on past Mill Road car park and then over Ditch End sluice before continuing along the bank above the tidal River Arun. The path gradually bends round to the north with good views back over the town and the castle and then swings west for another 500m to a sluice. Bear right past the sluice gates and then take the footpath off left through light

Arundel and Swanbourne Lake

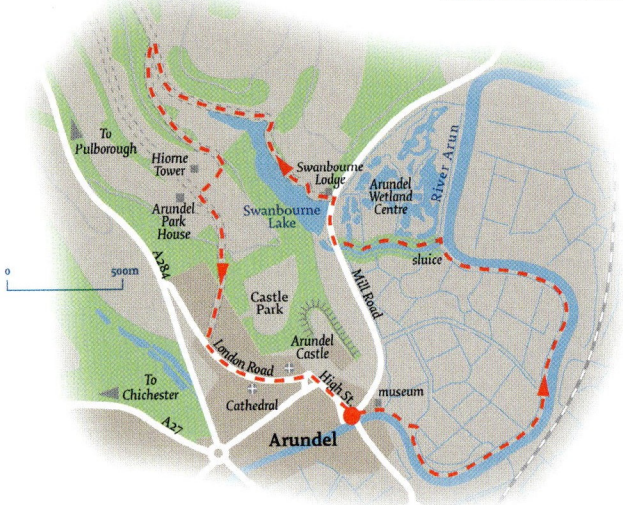

woodland along the southern edge of Arundel Wetland Centre to Mill Road.

Cross the road and bear right along it for 200m to the entrance to Swanbourne Lake at Swanbourne Lodge. The route now heads through the entrance, past the tearooms and along the path on the lake's northern side. The lake was originally a mill pond and features in John Constable's 1837 painting *Arundel Mill and Castle*. Today, it is a haven for wildlife and there are also rowing boats for hire. The path rises a little through the trees above the lake and then descends to a gate at its northwestern end. Continue along the valley path beyond for 400m up round the right bend to a prominent junction with a bridleway.

Here, the route turns sharp left onto the bridleway and climbs steadily for 600m above the steep-sided valley to a gate. Go through the gate and turn immediately right up steps and across the grass in front of the Hiorne Tower, a triangular structure with octagonal corner towers. The tower was built in the 1780s by the architect Francis Hiorne for the 11th Duke of Norfolk as an example of Gothic revival style in advance of planned restoration of the main castle. However, Hiorne never received the commission for the restoration and he died soon afterwards. At the surfaced byway beyond, turn left and follow it downhill to the gate into Castle Park. Continue ahead down the byway to London Road, where a left turn takes you past the cathedral to the top of the High Street. Bear right down the steep High Street alongside the castle wall to return to the start.

◀ Swanbourne Lake

Burpham

Distance 7.75km **Time** 2 hours 15
Terrain downland tracks and lanes
Map OS Explorer OL10 **Access** no public transport to the start

This walk takes you from a Saxon village up onto the downs where the field and path edges teem with flowers and insect life in spring and summer.

The walk begins from the small village of Burpham, which lies to the east of Arundel across the floodplain of the River Arun on the edge of the downs. Parking is available in the village car park opposite the church, down the rough lane behind The George pub. There is a good view southwards from here, past the cricket pitch over Burpham's Saxon burgh, an elongated promontory situated high above the River Arun and at one time fortified against Viking raids.

St Mary's Church dates back to the 11th century and in a blocked doorway in the nave has some stained glass which commemorates Edward Edwardes, an RAF pilot who died on active service in 1928. His father was Tickner Edwardes, who became vicar of Burpham in the late 1920s and was a published authority on honey bees. He is buried in the churchyard with his wife Kathleen. Buried nearby is the novelist and painter Mervyn Peake, likewise with his wife Maeve, also a writer and painter.

From the entrance to the church, walk past The George down through the village, round the left bend and along to the junction with Peppering Lane by Splash Farm Barn. Take the hedged bridleway ahead which rises steadily for just over 1km to Burpham High Barn. Continue past the barn and descend

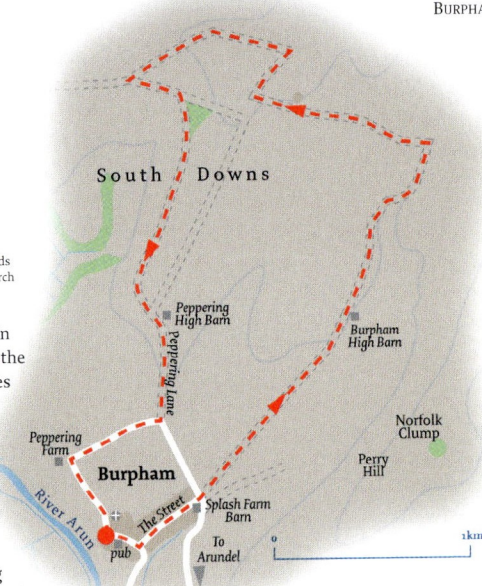

◀ In Burpham looking towards the tower of St Mary's Church

across a dip up to a bridleway junction. In spring and summer, the verges and field edges abound with wildflowers. The land here belongs to the Norfolk Estate and it has created a habitat in which nature can flourish by replacing winter sowing with spring sowing and leaving hedge and field boundaries unsprayed.

A left turn takes you up the bridleway track over a rise and across a dip to the next junction, where you turn right. After 200m, you pass a tumulus on your right – a raised section of the bank marks the spot and you can gain a glimpse of the barrow over the hedge. After another 50m, the route turns left onto a restricted byway and heads downhill for just under 1km, with a view ahead of Glatting Beacon, to a junction by a gate at the head of the lane up from North Stoke.

Turn sharp left here and follow the bridleway down round a bend, over a slight rise and gently downhill for a little under 1km to the flint walls of Peppering High Barn. Along this section are views over the Arun Valley, which in medieval times was known as 'the great wanderer' on account of its propensity to spread out over its floodplain. However, since the coming of the railway line to the valley in the 19th century the river's course has been straightened, though in wet winters it still floods.

The final part of the route follows Peppering Lane for 500m to a junction by a small grassy triangle and forks right down to Peppering Farm. Go round the left bend here and continue along the lane for the final 400m back to the church.

Storrington and Kithurst Hill

Distance 6km **Time** 1 hour 45
Terrain lanes, fields and open downland, with some steep gradients
Map OS Explorer OL10 **Access** bus to Storrington from Horsham and Burgess Hill, Worthing and Midhurst

Pick a clear day for this hike onto the South Downs and the reward will be some panoramic views.

The walk starts from the large village of Storrington, where long-stay parking is available on North Street or along the route on Orchard Gardens, opposite St Mary's Church. The busy A283 runs through the town centre and gives easy access to the South Downs, whose northern escarpment rises steeply above fields to the south of the village.

From the centre of Storrington, head down Church Street and, just after St Mary's Church, turn right along School Lane for 500m to the junction by Our Lady of England Priory. This was formerly the home of a community of Roman Catholic priests of the Premonstratensian order, also known as the White Canons, and is now a centre for retreats organised by the Chemin Neuf Community. In 1908 one of the priory's visitors was the writer Hilaire Belloc. Keep ahead up Kithurst Lane, which carries a footpath, and at the end of the lane by houses look out for a marker post. Here, the footpath forks left alongside a fence and continues gently downhill between fields and over two footbridges to a field gate.

Head up the field beyond for 400m to a stile into a second field and follow the path along the field edge. Once past the house named Coldharbour, the footpath leaves the field edge and bears left onto

The wooden Moorish gateway of St Joseph's Dominican Convent on the corner of Browns Lane and Church Street

the driveway, continuing to a junction with a bridleway at the bend. Fork right onto the bridleway which bends round to the right to reach a second bridleway junction. Take the left-hand of two bridleways steeply up the wooded escarpment for an ascent of just over 100m in height to a bridleway junction at the top of the down. A left turn for 500m now takes you more gently up to the triangulation pillar on top of Kithurst Hill, where there are extensive views northwards over the Weald to the North Downs and southwards to the Channel and the Isle of Wight.

The onward route descends through a gate into Access Land and continues ahead for 250m down to a junction with a bridleway at the head of the combe of Chantry Hill. Turn left down the bridleway around the head of the combe and descend the northern spur of the hill for another 250m to a marker post at a path junction a little above the treeline. Here, make sure you bear left to stay on the bridleway, which winds down through the wooded combe on the northern side of Kithurst Hill to Greyfriars Farm. Continue down the farm track, which carries the bridleway, and then keep ahead along Greyfriars Lane for another 700m to St Mary's Church. From here, head back along Church Street to the start.

Bramber and Annington Hill

Distance 10km **Time** 2 hours 45
Terrain riverside path, lanes and open downland **Maps** OS Explorer OL10 & OL11
Access bus to Bramber from Brighton, Rottingdean and Burgess Hill

Stride out alongside the River Adur and over the downs on this longer circuit from an historic village.

The walk starts from the village of Bramber, where parking is available in the car park off The Street in the middle of the village or by Bramber Castle. At the western edge of the village are the Church of St Nicholas and the ruins of Bramber Castle, constructed shortly after the Norman conquest as the Sussex seat of the de Braose family. In the centre of the village you'll find St Mary's House, which was built in the 15th century as an inn for pilgrims on their way to Canterbury. Both the castle and St Mary's House are open to the public.

Walk along The Street towards the eastern end of the village to the timber-framed St Mary's House and take the surfaced footpath off right past its entrance. The footpath bends left to a junction with the path alongside the River Adur. Turn right and for the next 1.5km follow the riverside path, which passes under the A283 and then continues to the junction with the South Downs Way. Turn right here onto the South Downs Way, which is followed for the middle part of the walk, and head along to Annington Road. Here, it's worth the short detour left for 200m along the lane to St Botolph's Church. The building is of Saxon origin and was known as 'the Wayfarers Church' as it served as a refuge for pilgrims at the crossing point of the River Adur on

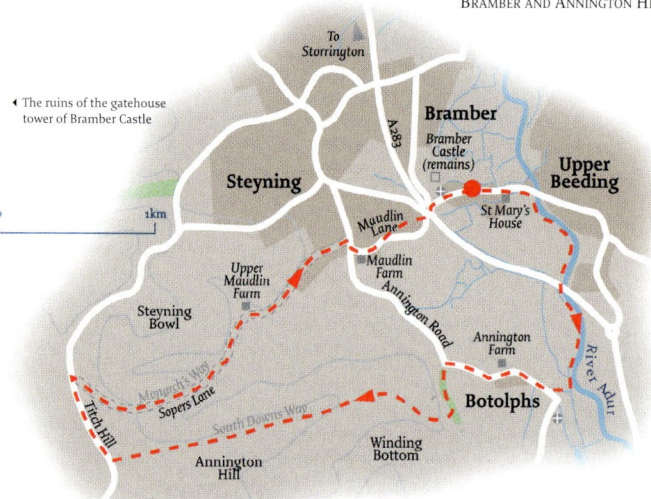

◀ The ruins of the gatehouse tower of Bramber Castle

the route now followed by the South Downs Way.

The onward route turns right on a path parallel to the road to the next bend and then climbs the twisting lane up through the village of Botolphs past the entrance to Annington House. Just beyond, at the sharp right bend, look out for the South Downs Way fingerpost directing you off left up the wooded track to Tinpots. Here, the South Downs Way turns right and climbs more steeply up out of the trees. It's a steady climb for a little over 2km across the open downs with good views right over Steyning Bowl and up to Bostal Road which runs along the ridge. At the road, the Way turns right along a path parallel to the road for 600m to the junction with Sopers Lane, which carries a bridleway and the Monarch's Way.

Here, you leave the South Downs Way and turn right onto the Monarch's Way, which is followed for the final part of the route, down the surfaced track to Sopers Bottom and then up over the rise to Upper Maudlyn Farm. The Monarch's Way continues along the lane ahead uphill and then down to the junction with Annington Road. A short dogleg right, then left along Maudlin Lane takes you to Maudlin Farm. Just beyond its buildings, where the lane heads downhill, turn left onto a footpath up a few steps and then bear to the right diagonally down a field to the bottom of Maudlin Lane by the roundabout. Cross over Maudlin Lane and then the A283 and head along The Street back to the centre of Bramber, along which you pass the turning up to the Church of St Nicholas and Bramber Castle.

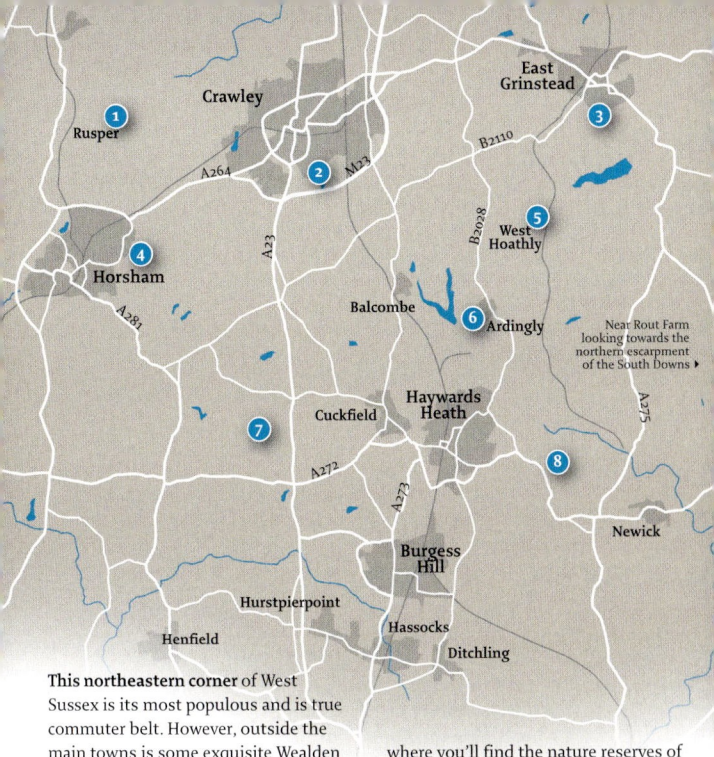

Near Rout Farm looking towards the northern escarpment of the South Downs

This northeastern corner of West Sussex is its most populous and is true commuter belt. However, outside the main towns is some exquisite Wealden countryside, within easy reach of the M23 and the main railway lines from London.

West of Crawley and just a stroll from the village of Rusper lies the source of the River Mole, which flows northwards to the Surrey Hills on its way to the Thames, while to the southeast of the town, tucked inside the curve of the M23 motorway, is Tilgate Park, the town's extensive green space.

Busy Horsham is limited by ancient St Leonard's Forest on its eastern fringe, where you'll find the nature reserves of Leechpool and Owlbeech Woods. To the south, the quiet villages of Bolney and Warninglid seem at odds with the nearby roar of the now widened A23.

Further east near the county border, the historic market town of East Grinstead makes a good starting point for a longer stroll to Weir Wood Reservoir. South towards Haywards Heath is a less-visited pocket of rolling countryside containing the pretty Wealden villages of West Hoathly, Ardingly and Scaynes Hill.

Crawley, Horsham and Haywards Heath

1 **Rusper and the River Mole** 80
Begin near the memorial to a pioneer of the English folk music revival to explore some inspirational countryside

2 **Tilgate Park** 82
This short route is perfect for walking the dog, entertaining the kids or just relaxing afterwards by the lake

3 **East Grinstead and Weir Wood Reservoir** 84
Call in at the Arts and Crafts house of Standen on this delightful tour of fields and woodland

4 **Leechpool and Owlbeech Woods** 86
Look out for the cattle, sheep and horses that help to maintain the woodland and heathland habitat on this waymarked walk

5 **West Hoathly and the Gravetye Estate** 88
There's plenty to see in the pretty village of West Hoathly, including the 15th-century Priest House

6 **Ardingly** 90
This short stroll is best combined with a visit to nearby Wakehurst, known as 'Kew in the country'

7 **Bolney and Warninglid** 92
Set out along the High Weald Landscape Trail on this hilly route and let the Sussex Diamond Way guide you home

8 **Scaynes Hill** 94
Medieval labourers once worked these ancient fields just a short distance from busy Haywards Heath

Rusper and the River Mole

Distance 7.5km **Time** 2 hours
Terrain fields and woodland
Map OS Explorer OL34 **Access** no public transport to the start

Ramble through woods and fields and meander alongside the infant River Mole.

From the centre of Rusper, walk up the High Street to St Mary Magdalene Church and the Parish Council car park, where a panel outside the church celebrates the life of Lucy Broadwood, a collector of English folk songs during the late 19th and early 20th centuries. She is buried here and there is a memorial to her inside the church. Continue ahead along the hedged walkway which runs parallel with the road for 150m to the football field. Turn left with the Sussex Border Path along the edge of the pitch and continue down the field beyond into Horsegills Wood. The Sussex Border Path heads gently down through the trees and, after 300m, bends right down across a footbridge in a dell. Climb the far side and bear right to a gate into fields.

Still following the Sussex Border Path, turn left along field edges, then head back into the wood and continue beside a stream to a stile on the right into fields after 350m. Cross the stile, bear right up to a second stile in the hedge and then turn left to Porter's Farm. Just beyond the buildings, look out for the fingerpost showing the way over the next two fields to Friday Street.

Turn left along Friday Street through the hamlet and after just over 100m by Friday Farm, where the Sussex Border Path heads off right, take the footpath to

◀ St Mary Magdalene Church, Rusper

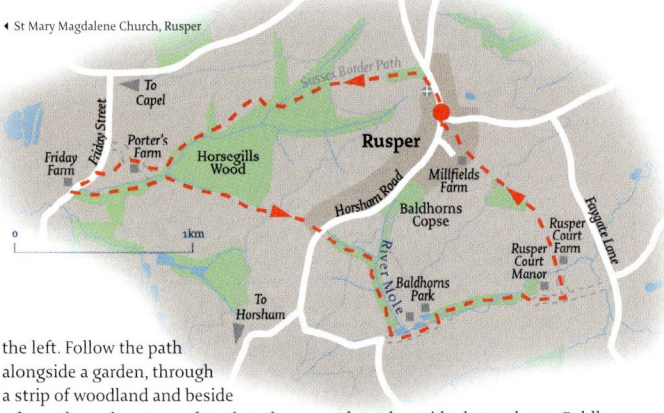

the left. Follow the path alongside a garden, through a strip of woodland and beside a fence through an area of scrub and field-edge brambles. The footpath then joins a hedged track and passes along the southern edge of Horsegills Wood, up between fields and over the rise to Horsham Road.

Dogleg left, then right across the road and follow the left edge of the large field beyond down to its far right corner. The path enters woodland, crosses a small footbridge and heads alongside the infant River Mole, a short distance from its source to the north in Baldhorns Copse. The river here is flowing southwards, though for most of its length it flows northwards to the River Thames. At the end of the wood continue down alongside the fence, with Baldhorns Park on the left, to a bridleway junction and driveway.

Turn left and follow the bridleway down the driveway of Baldhorns Park and then alongside the track past Baldhorns Park Farm. Just beyond, the bridleway crosses the River Mole and then passes along a field edge and through woodland to a footbridge. Cross back over the River Mole and continue along the bridleway beside the river, through a patch of woodland and then alongside a field to the driveway of Rusper Court Manor. Bear right along the driveway for 50m and then take the footpath off left up the driveway to East and West Riverside cottages.

Here, the route forks left across the River Mole one final time and up the edge of the field beyond. After 350m, just before a copse, cross a small footbridge on the right. At the path junction after this, bear left and head up two fields to Millfields Farm. Keep ahead on a fenced walkway along the backs of gardens and past the car park of the Star Inn to Horsham Road and the village centre.

Tilgate Park

Distance 3.5km **Time** 1 hour
Terrain lakeside and woodland paths
Map OS Explorer OL34 **Access** bus (Metrobus) from Crawley to Tilgate Park (weekends and Bank Holidays only) or to K2 Leisure Centre near the bottom of Tilgate Drive, 1km from the main car park (Monday to Friday)

Enjoy the varied terrain of this popular country estate just a short distance from busy Crawley.

The walk starts from the main car park in Tilgate Park, which is located on Tilgate Drive on the southern edge of Crawley. The park, open to the public since 1978, comprises lakes, gardens and woodland, and is managed by Crawley Borough Council. Originally a country estate, there is now a nature centre, a children's play area, a walled garden, which is one of the remaining features of the Tilgate Estate and now houses a café, and a watersports centre by Tilgate Lake, where canoes, rowing boats, pedalos and also bikes are available for hire. Dogs are welcome in the park but are not permitted in the nature centre, the children's play area or the walled garden.

From the car park, follow signs to the play area and head down the grass to Tilgate Lake. Turn left past the watersports centre and then the outdoor gym to the northern end of the lake and bear right on the walkway around its head. At the far side, bend right with the surfaced path and follow it down the eastern side. At the southern end of the lake, where the path bends right between Tilgate and Silt Lakes, keep ahead for 100m onto a forest path up past an area of open heath on the left to a path junction. Fork right and continue through the trees to the T-junction at the foot of the embankment of the M23 motorway.

You now turn right and after 75m, at the

◀ The northern end of Tilgate Lake

first fork in the path, keep left and then, in another 75m at a second fork, keep right onto a wide path. Follow this for the next 300m as it curves around a couple of ponds in a dell on the left to a junction with a track called The Avenue. Turn right onto The Avenue uphill for 100m and then bend round to the right up this broad forestry path to a crosspaths at the top of the rise. Continue downhill for 300m to a small stream in the dip and just beyond look out for a path on the right.

Turn right along the path through the trees and then, with Titmus Lake a little off to the right, keep ahead along the main path for 200m towards the recreation centre. Continue alongside its fence and bend round to the right to a fork in the path, where you keep right onto the path which crosses the head of Titmus Lake. On the far side, a short dogleg right, then left takes you uphill along the path between the heather garden and the nature centre. At the top of the rise, you pass the entrance to the nature centre and the walled garden. To return to the start, turn left and follow the signs back downhill for 250m to the main car park.

East Grinstead and Weir Wood Reservoir

Distance 12km **Time** 3 hours 30
Terrain streets, fields, woodland and lanes; sections can be muddy in wet conditions **Map** OS Explorer 135
Access bus to East Grinstead from Brighton, Tunbridge Wells and Uckfield

Stride out across the countryside from an historic market town on this loop along waymarked trails.

From the High Street in the centre of East Grinstead, head past the war memorial and the wooden-framed Clarendon House and fork right down West Street for 700m past the library to the roundabout at the bottom of the hill. Continue for 30m along Turners Hill Road opposite and turn left with the High Weald Landscape Trail, which is followed to Weir Wood Reservoir.

For the next 1km the Landscape Trail passes along the backs of houses beside a brook, along the edges of four fields and between the houses on Streatfield Place to West Hoathly Road. Turn right up the pavement for just over 100m and then go right onto the footpath along Coombe Hill Road. After 200m, turn left along Medway Drive past houses into fields. From here, the Landscape Trail heads up the valley along the edges of five fields to a junction with a bridleway by the playing field of East Grinstead Rugby Club.

Turn left along the side of the pitches and past the communications mast to the road. Dogleg left for 30m, then right and follow the footpath along the lane to Standen for 300m to a path junction on the right opposite the entrance to Rockinghills Wood. If you wish to visit Standen, the National Trust-owned Arts and Crafts house with William Morris-decorated interiors, or its Barn Café, you can continue for 200m down the entrance road.

The onward route turns right off the

◀ Looking north from near Busses Farm towards East Grinstead

lane and heads along a fenced path beside fields for 350m to a gate. Follow the left edge of the field beyond and head down through woodland to a fork in the path. Keep left and descend one more field to reach the fence that runs along the northern side of Weir Wood Reservoir. Turn left and follow the Sussex Border Path along field edges and through sections of woodland. In 1km, the Sussex Border Path veers left, then right through Busses Wood before passing a small picnic area on the right, with a view over the reservoir. Continue for another 100m to a path junction.

Here, turn left with the Sussex Border Path up alongside a field and then a track to Busses Farm. Head to the left of the cowsheds and dogleg right, then left between a pond and the farmhouse to the start of a byway. The Border Path forks right here onto a bridleway for the next 1km and heads down three fields, crosses a footbridge and continues up to a junction with a track by a house. Turn left up the track for 400m and, just before the bridge over the disused railway, fork right down to the old trackbed of the East Grinstead to Tunbridge Wells railway and turn left along the linear Forest Way Country Park. Follow this shared-use route for the next 2km up the gentle incline, cross over Herontye Drive and, after another 100m, fork left up to Lewes Road. Here, a left turn will take you up the pavement back to the High Street.

Leechpool and Owlbeech Woods

Distance 3km **Time** 1 hour
Terrain woodland paths and tracks; sections can be muddy
Map OS Explorer OL34 **Access** no public transport to the start

Explore a typical West Sussex woodland and heath on the edge of the Weald Forest Ridge.

The walk starts from Leechpool Woods car park, off Harwood Road on the eastern edge of Horsham. The site comprises 110 acres of heathland, woodland and wetland. Admission is free and the woods are open all year round. Dogs are welcome and the terrain can be muddy. There are five signposted walking trails around the ancient woodland of Leechpool Woods and the restored heathland in Owlbeech Woods, which is grazed by cattle, sheep and horses. This walk combines two of the marked trails, the Woodland Walk and the Heathland Walk.

Head out the southern side of the car park and turn left towards the picnic area, where there is an information panel. The first part of the walk follows the yellow arrows of the waymarked Woodland Walk. These take you past the picnic area and through Leechpool Woods on a wide path, which bends to the right and then back left to reach the far edge of the wood by a children's play area. Turn right past an outdoor basketball court down to a second information panel.

The route now joins the Heathland Walk, which is waymarked by purple arrows. Turn left past the panel into

◂ Middle Heath in Owlbeech Wood

Owlbeech Wood and follow the wide, mostly level path northeastwards with a stream down on the right. After 400m, the Heathland Walk bends right down across the stream. A short climb brings you out of the trees up to a bend by the edge of the heathland. The Heathland Walk now bends left along the northern edge of Middle Heath for 200m and then bears right uphill. After 150m, keep on the main path as it bends right up along the southern edge of Middle Heath. You gradually descend and then cross the dip of Alder Gill. Continue up the far side for another 100m to a path junction.

Here, you turn sharp right onto a path that leads between enclosures, past a sculpted bench and down steps back into woodland. The Heathland Walk now doglegs left for 100m, then right across a footbridge over the stream and up the far side for 50m to a fork in the path. Bear left here and rejoin the Woodland Walk, which heads through the trees past a pond to a path junction. Continue straight ahead and after 200m pass along a section of boardwalk and then, a little further on, over a crosspaths to reach a footbridge. Cross the footbridge and carry on uphill for 100m to reach the path taken on the outward route, where a left turn will take you back to the picnic area and car park.

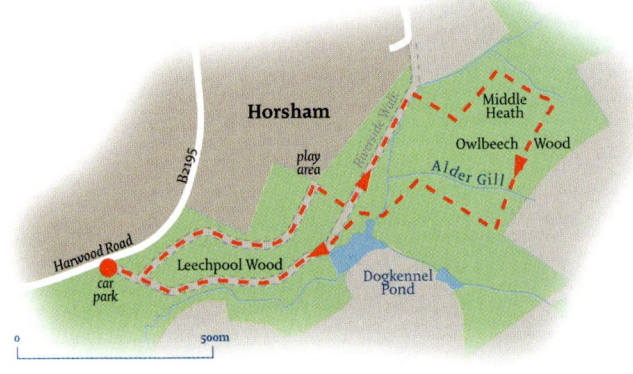

West Hoathly and the Gravetye Estate

Distance 6km **Time** 1 hour 45
Terrain fields, lanes and woodland paths
Map OS Explorer 135 **Access** bus to West Hoathly from Crawley and East Grinstead (limited service)

This circuit loops around an estate once owned by the Irish gardener William Robinson, who was a pioneer of the natural-looking garden.

The walk starts from the village of West Hoathly, where parking is available in the village and on its eastern edge off Church Hill in Finche Field car park. In the village is The Priest House, an open hall house built in 1430 by Lewes Priory. Since 1908, it has been a museum and is open to the public from March to October. The Church of St Margaret is more than 900 years old and from the churchyard there is an outstanding view over the South Downs. Inside is an impressive Geometric window, whose design was copied from an example in the French city of Angers.

From the area known as Queen's Square, the centre of the village, by St Margaret's Church and The Cat Inn, walk up to the far end of North Lane on the route of the High Weald Landscape Trail, which is followed for the first half of the walk. At the junction, cross over onto the footpath past West Hoathly Garage and along a driveway past gardens. After 250m, go through a gate, continue down a sunken path for another 100m and fork left into fields by a Gravetye Estate sign.

Head down two fields before continuing down into woodland to a path junction. Keep ahead out of the wood and along the edge of the next field, at the end of which you bend left down into woodland again to a footbridge. Cross the bridge and head uphill to the driveway of Gravetye Manor. Now a hotel, it was built as a private home

WEST HOATHLY AND THE GRAVETYE ESTATE

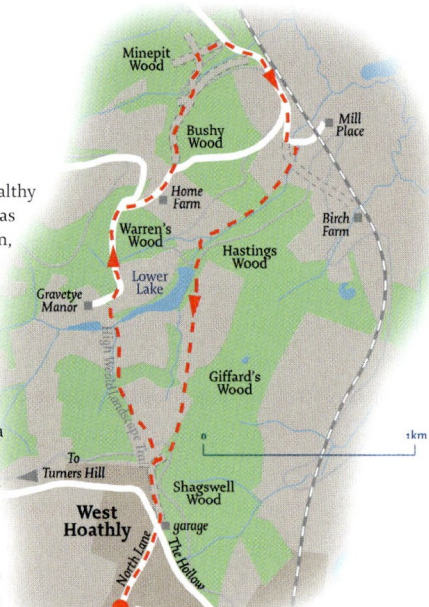

◀ The Priest House, West Hoathly

in 1598 by Richard Infield, a wealthy Sussex ironmaster. In 1884 it was purchased by William Robinson, who revolutionised the art of gardening and is credited with introducing the herbaceous border and the 'wild' garden.

Head up the driveway for 300m and, just round the right bend, make sure you fork right with the Landscape Trail onto a track. You now descend past some farm cottages and continue along the track for another 150m to a right bend. Here, the Landscape Trail forks left past a metal barrier up into Bushy Wood, climbs over a rise and then bends round to the right. Keep on downhill, over a crosspaths and across a stream. The trail soon bends left under electricity wires and after another 100m reaches a prominent crosspaths. Go right here for just over 100m to a narrow lane, which carries a bridleway.

Turn right along the lane for 600m down across a dip, over a rise and then down past cottages to the entrance to Birch Farm. There is no right of way ahead along the farm track, so dogleg left with the bridleway for 30m, then right off the High Weald Landscape Trail onto a footpath which leads back over the farm track and into fields. Follow the footpath over the first field, through a stand of woodland and along the edges of two more fields. In the third field turn left with the footpath up through the wood to Lower Lake. Continue past the lake, beyond which the footpath heads uphill for the next 800m over three fields. Rejoin the outward route back up the sunken lane to North Lane and the village centre.

Ardingly

Distance 5.5km **Time** 1 hour 30
Terrain lanes, path beside reservoir, woods and fields **Map** OS Explorer 135
Access bus to Ardingly from Haywards Heath and Brighton (limited service)

This hands-in-pockets stroll saunters along lanes and over fields to the edge of Ardingly Reservoir.

The walk starts from the centre of the village of Ardingly at the junction of the High Street with Street Lane, where there is a car park. To the west of the village lies Ardingly Reservoir, which was built in 1979 by damming the Shell Brook, a tributary of the River Ouse. The reservoir has been designated a Local Nature Reserve and is popular with anglers, canoeists and sailors. The village also attracts visitors to Wakehurst, which lies a short distance to the north. This famous 500-acre garden, which also houses the Millennium Seed Bank, is managed by the Royal Botanic Gardens, Kew and is part of the National Trust.

Walk along the pavement of Street Lane for just under 1km past houses to the junction at the western end of the village by St Peter's Church, which has an unusual 16th-century timbered porch at the south door, with wooden weatherboarding and a roof tiled with Horsham stone slabs. Turn left down Church Lane to the end of the public road, where a footpath continues ahead along a private road. After 200m, the road becomes a track and bends right to a footpath junction by the buildings of Townhouse Farm. Continue ahead past the farm buildings and along the track down through woodland into fields. Follow the edges of two fields down to Ardingly Reservoir.

A left turn takes you onto the path

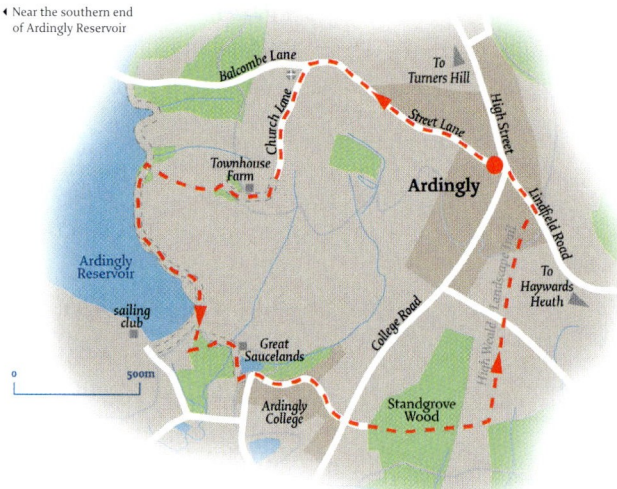

◀ Near the southern end of Ardingly Reservoir

alongside the reservoir's edge towards its southern end. After 500m, follow the path up into the trees and round to the right to the dam wall. From here, you can detour across the dam to the sailing club on the far side, which has a seasonal refreshment kiosk. The onward route forks left down the grass bank and, just before the car park, turns left through a gate into woodland onto the High Weald Landscape Trail. Head through the trees for just over 100m to a path junction at a driveway. Turn right onto the footpath along the driveway past Great Saucelands and alongside a small lake to the buildings of Ardingly College. The Landscape Trail now follows the right of way, a bridleway, through the college buildings, where it heads up the hill, bends left and then back right past the cricket pitches to the entrance.

Cross College Road and follow the Landscape Trail along the footpath through Standgrove Wood. Continue across the field beyond to a crosspaths on the far side, where the trail turns left along the field edge. Follow the footpath up the middle of the next two fields, along the edge of a fourth and down a driveway to Lindfield Road. Here, leave the Landscape Trail and turn left along the pavement for 200m to return to the centre of Ardingly.

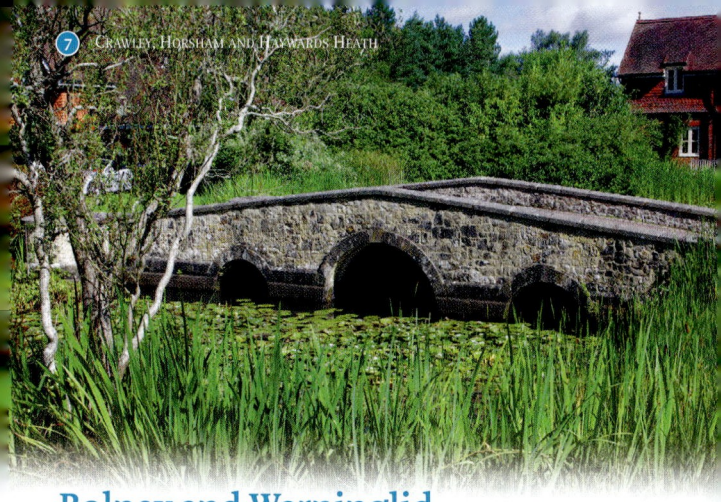

Bolney and Warninglid

Distance 8km **Time** 2 hours 15
Terrain woodland, parkland and fields
Map OS Explorer OL34 **Access** bus to
Bolney from Haywards Heath

Head over the ridge that lies between two picturesque Mid-Sussex villages and enjoy the views on the return.

The walk starts from the northern end of the village of Bolney at the junction of The Street with Ryecroft Road by the war memorial. Parking is available on The Street. Walk up to the top of The Street, on the route of the High Weald Landscape Trail. Where the lane bends right into Top Street, keep ahead onto a footpath up a track to a gate at the edge of Wykehurst Park. Continue with the Landscape Trail uphill into woodland along a sunken path, under a bridge and up to a crosspaths. Carry on over the rise and descend past a pylon down through the woodland to a footbridge over a small stream at its northern edge. From here, follow the waymarks uphill through parkland, across a driveway and up the right-hand side of a field to Jeremys Lane.

The Landscape Trail now turns left and follows the lane up to the junction with Colwood Lane. Here, turn right along the lane past the entrance to Colwood Court and then Rout Farm, before following it down the northern side of Colwood Hill. At the bottom, the Landscape Trail continues along the lane through the bends and uphill for another 200m to a crosspaths by a modern house called Fernbreeze.

Leave the Landscape Trail here and turn left off the lane onto the footpath which heads along the edges of fields and through some small patches of woodland

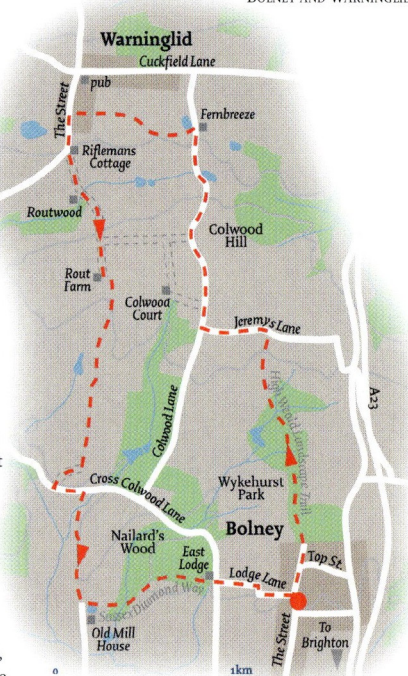

◀ The village pond in Warninglid

to The Street in Warninglid. You can make a short detour off right through the village to The Half Moon pub by the crossroads with Cuckfield Lane.

The return route turns left along The Street steeply down to the bend. Keep ahead here onto the bridleway past Riflemans Cottage, a former pub, down the drive to Routwood. The bridleway forks left in front of the house, crosses a stream and then climbs steeply up over the rise to the buildings of Rout Farm. The bridleway doglegs left between the buildings, then right and descends southwards for 1km between fields down to some cottages, where it bears to the right along the driveway down to Cross Colwood Lane. Turn left along the lane for 150m and take the footpath off right on the route of the Sussex Diamond Way, whose waymarks are followed for the rest of the walk.

The Diamond Way heads down between fields, through woodland and down a sunken path to a crosspaths by Old Mill House. Here, turn sharp left over a field, along a hedged section into woodland and across a footbridge to a path junction. The Diamond Way forks left up through a pine plantation, bends right past a pylon to the top of the rise and then descends to East Lodge on Cross Colwood Lane. Cross over and follow Lodge Lane back to The Street in Bolney.

Scaynes Hill

Distance 6km **Time** 1 hour 45
Terrain fields and woods
Map OS Explorer 135 **Access** bus to Scaynes Hill from Uckfield and Haywards Heath

Follow two waymarked trails on this undulating route over fields and past old farms.

The walk starts from the car park on Scaynes Hill Common, which is located 500m along Church Road to the north of Scaynes Hill, a small village 3km east of Haywards Heath. The village name has undergone a number of adaptions and in the 16th century was known as Skerns and in the 18th as Scarmes Hill. In medieval times, the name had been Heanfelde, from the Old English meaning 'high open land'. The common is a mix of acid and neutral grassland and today is managed like a traditional hay meadow by cutting annually in late summer. This encourages a beautiful and varied covering of grasses and flowers in spring and summer.

By the car park entrance, take the footpath that forks right (northwards) through the trees to the top of the common and bear right along a fenced path into fields along the route of the Sussex Ouse Valley Way, which is followed for the first half of the walk. Follow the waymarks down over three fields to a driveway and turn left down to the entrance to Pegden. The footpath forks left down a wooded track and then down the next field to a gate into woodland. Go through the gate and take the left fork down through the trees and along a fence to a footpath junction. Bear left across the next field to the driveway to Ham House

◀ Scaynes Hill Common in summer

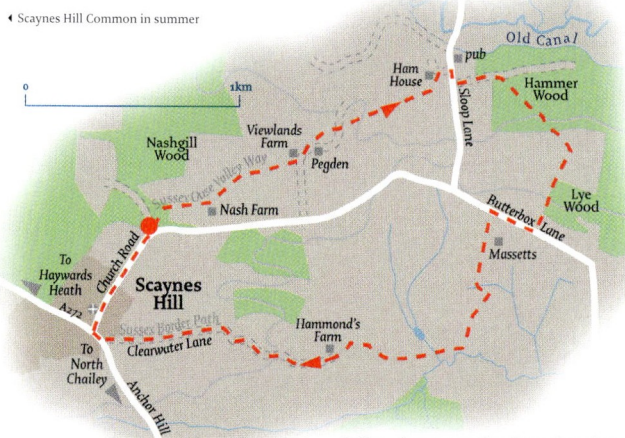

and turn right to Sloop Lane, which carries the Sussex Border Path and where you will find the Sloop Inn down to the left near the River Ouse.

The onward route turns right with both waymarked trails up the lane for 50m and then left onto a footpath along a track past cottages to a wooden barrier in Hammer Wood. Here, fork right up through the wood to the gate at the top and cross the field beyond to a footpath junction. Leave the Sussex Ouse Valley Way here and turn right with the Sussex Border Path.

This follows a track over two small fields, forks left down the edge of Lye Wood and continues down a track to Butterbox Lane. Dogleg right for 200m up the lane and, just past a house called Massetts, turn left into fields again. Follow the waymarks along the edges of two fields, up over the rise in the third field and down to a gate in the dip by a line of oak trees. Turn right across the fourth field and, in the fifth, head across to the far side and then turn right up its edge to the top of the rise by a corner of woodland. Here, the Sussex Border Path doglegs right back across the field and then left along the far edge towards Hammonds Farm. Pass to the left of the farm to its driveway.

The footpath now heads left for 1km along the twisting driveway, uphill through a sharp left bend and along past Oakgates Farm to the A272 at Scaynes Hill. Turn right past the service station and then right along Church Road to the junction with Vicarage Lane, beyond which a path leads over the edge of the common back to the car park.

Index

Adur, River	56, 58, 76
Arun, River	66, 68, 70, 72
Amberley	68
Annington Hill	76
Ardingly	90
Arundel	30, 70, 72
Beacon Hill	20
Bevis's Thumb	26
Bignor	62
Black Down	8, 20
Bolney	92
Bramber	76
Burpham	72
Butser Hill	26
Bury	68
Byworth	52
Charlton	28
Chichester	36
Chidham	38
Cocking	22
Compton	26
Crawley	82
East Grinstead	84
East Harting	20
East Lavant	34
Glatting Beacon	72
Graveyte Estate	88
Haslemere	8
Henfield	58
High Titten	68
Hiorne Tower	70
Horsham	86, 90
Iping	12, 14
Kingley Vale	32
Kithurst Hill	74
Knepp Castle Estate	56
Lavant, River	28, 34
Leechpool Woods	86
Littlehampton	66
Lodsworth	18
Loxwood	46
Midhurst	14, 16, 22, 34
Mole, River	80
Northchapel	44
Older Hill	10
Owlbeech Woods	86
Pen Hill	20
Petworth	52
Pitshill	18
Pulborough Brooks	54
Rother, River	16
Rowlands Castle	30
Rudgwick	48
Rusper	80
Scaynes Hill	94
Singleton	28
Slindon	64
South Harting	20
Stansted Park	30
Stedham	12, 14
Storrington	74
Sussex Border Path	8
Sutton	62
Swanbourne Lake	70
Tansley Stone	32
Temple of the Winds, The	8
Tilgate	82
Tillington	18
Titty Hill	10
Upperton	18
Warninglid	92
Weir Wood Reservoir	84
Westburton Hill	62
West Dean	22, 34
West Hoathly	88
West Itchenor	40
West Stoke	32
Wey & Arun Canal	46, 50
Wisborough Green	50
Witley Copse	8
Woolbeding	10